Dancing

A FORD FOUNDATION REPORT

by Elizabeth Kendall

One of a series of reports on activities supported by the Ford Foundation. A complete list of publications may be obtained from the Ford Foundation, Office of Reports, 320 East 43 Street, New York, N.Y. 10017.

Library of Congress Cataloging in Publication Data
Kendall, Elizabeth, 1947–
  Dancing.

  (A Ford Foundation report)
  Free single copies only.
    1. Ballet — United States — History.   2. Dancing — United States — Finance.   3. Ford Foundation — Endowments.
I. Ford Foundation.   II. Title.   III. Series.
GV1623.K457   1983   792.8'0973   83-11622

December 1983   X-37

Contents

Introduction

In the late nineteenth century, a brash and newly prosperous America set out to acquire for itself the civilized arts of Europe. Wealthy Americans began buying up European paintings, sculptures, furniture, even castles, and bringing them home. Businessmen in New York and Chicago founded great opera theaters where they could view, on home turf, the cream of French, German, and Italian productions, sung by an amalgam of European and American singers.

But ballet, an art of impeccable classical-Renaissance origins, did not readily lend itself to transplantation. This art, to be whole and effective, required an entire company of dancers and an academy to train them—and not even the most ambitious robber-baron thought of importing that much. In nineteenth-century Europe, moreover, ballet's reputation as a fine art was not secure. In England and France it was thought of as light entertainment, in a class with the pantomime and the operetta and practiced almost exclusively by females assumed to be of questionable virtue.

Only in Russia was ballet healthy, alive, and evolving, so much so that in 1909, when Serge Diaghilev's Russian Ballet burst upon an astonished Paris, audiences barely recognized it as ballet. There were *men* dancing on the Russian's stage—a new, fierce, expressive kind of dancing fashioned out of the classic ballet tradition but infused with the wild new colors of the Russian painters who designed the décors and the exuberant, sometimes cacophonous music of the young composers who wrote the scores. The intellectual elite of London and Paris took to the Ballets Russes with almost fanatical interest. The art so brilliantly presented by Diaghilev seemed to capture the exhilaration of the age.

The story of ballet in this century is the story of how that dynamic first impulse in Russia spread to other countries, including the United States, and took hold in them. It is the story of how Russian expatriates revitalized the teaching of ballet in countries where it had languished—in France, for example—and created ballet traditions where, as in England or this country, none had previously existed.

Though dance in America is not limited to ballet, it was ballet that in the late fifties received the initial support of the Ford Foundation in the area of dance. When the Foundation first surveyed the field of concert dance, which was then split between modern dance and ballet, it saw a need to concentrate first and foremost on the problem of dance training and its link with the professional stage.

...by "classic" dance I mean a system of fundamental instruction for dancing comparable to an understanding of cadence, harmony and counterpoint in music; form, value and color in paint; structure, material and function in architecture. Tradition only means a handing down. Great dancers, ballet-masters, musicians and costumers have each and every one added their individual contributions, as in the brother dynasties of physicians, architects and poets.

LINCOLN KIRSTEIN, *Blast at Ballet* (1938)

Modern dance, though it contained many dynamic dances and dance idioms created by American choreographers, had not fostered professional schools to serve the whole dance field. Instead, modern dance academies fed individual companies. But such specialized training methods—training in anticipation of rehearsal and performance—were normal in this young branch of the art. After all, the idea of modern dance, the concept of a whole dance language made up from scratch by one person, had only existed since 1906, when Isadora Duncan started her first school in Germany.

In ballet, traditions dating back to the sixteenth century ensured that a good school could provide its students with a neutral base of expertise, a knowledge of the ballet grammar, that ballet choreographers could take and bend to their individual ends much as writers use a language of words and shape it to *their* ends.

The trouble was that there were few good ballet schools in the United States. Even as late as 1957, a national pattern of ballet training was difficult to discern. Some schools were not qualified to bring students to a professional level. The leading ballet academy in the country was the School of American Ballet in New York City, founded in 1934 by George Balanchine, who as a young man in the late 1920s had been Diaghilev's last ballet master and choreographer, and by Lincoln Kirstein, a young American connoisseur of the arts who had sponsored Balanchine's arrival out of his passionate desire to see classical ballet take root in this country.

In the late fifties the Ford Foundation, with the help of the School of American Ballet and consulting experts from around the country, devised a program to support teachers who could train ballet professionals to dance in companies and the companies with which such teachers were connected. In 1959 the program was implemented. Today, after twenty-four years, the Ford Foundation is understood to have had a substantial impact on the state of dance around the country today.

There is a wealth of dance activity in America. In the past two decades alone, ballet has spread far enough and reached deep enough in the population to become a regular part of the cultural life of almost every region. Standards of training have been widely recognized, private patrons and government agencies have emerged to support some full-time artist-professionals in the field, and the audience for dance has grown dramatically.

The following is an informal account of how ballet came to America, how it evolved and became known, what the Ford Foundation did to help develop the professional resources of performance and training in ballet, and what it later did in modern dance.

Background

Except for the dances of the American Indians, all our dancing was at first imported. With immigrants and slaves came all kinds of folk-dance forms to these shores—clog dances, jigs and reels, African rhythms—which, mingling and changing, sooner or later brought forth our own brand of popular theater dance to the stages of vaudeville and musical comedy. But in the late nineteenth century very little American-style "artistic" dancing was in evidence on the stage—dancing that might appeal to the higher sentiments. And no one knew what that style should be.

Codified dance was first brought to this country by foreign dancing masters, who taught the more genteel folk dances—schottisches, varsoviennes, mazurkas—along with gestures, a bit of pantomime, and sometimes morsels of ballet. They taught all over the country; many of them wandered from town to town with their memories of the dances of Italy or France or Bavaria or Jutland. They were like the émigré musicians who often settled alone in a town or a city and taught the children of pioneers how to play the piano or the violin. Whether they were highly accomplished or only moderately so, there is something remarkable in the efforts of these teachers to propagate Europe's music culture and its quaint formal dances in towns with muddy streets and wooden boards for sidewalks.

There were always certain small communities that prided themselves more than others on their art: the state of Utah boasted a few such communities. In the mid-nineteenth century, a family of music and dancing teachers named Christensen settled in Utah. The grandfather, Louis, converted to the Mormon religion, which, unlike most Protestant sects, strongly encouraged singing and dancing. The several sons of Louis Christensen grew up to be teachers of music and dancing (and deportment and whatever else was required) and one of them, Moes, went to New York in search of the developed dancing technique he knew must exist. He found an Italian maestro named Stefano Mascagno to teach him; one can imagine the wonderment of the small, dapper Mascagno at seeing this giant red-haired Dane from Utah at his door.

The Italian, Mascagno, soon joined the Christensens in Utah and inherited the next generation of Christensens as his students: nephews of Moes, the brothers Willam, Harold, and Lew. As the climate in America for serious ballet gradually improved, they, in turn, became almost the first American-born dancers and choreographers.

Right: *Lew Christensen in a 1937 American Ballet production of* Apollon Musagète, *an early Balanchine work with music by Stravinsky.* Below: *Dorothie (left) and Catherine Littlefield returning from a 1931 trip abroad in which they studied the work of several European dance companies.*

The evolution of the Christensen family shows how American ballet grew: the techniques of European dance masters and mistresses (who understood not only ballet disciplines but the social and cultural contexts in which they made sense) were worked into the physical identities of young Americans. The original Christensen, a European, brought his art culture with him; his sons and grandsons sought to replenish theirs from other Europeans: first Italians, and then Russians when they began to come to America.

A family just as significant to American ballet was the Littlefields. Caroline Littlefield had a ballet school in Philadelphia, and her daughters, Catherine and Dorothie, graduated from their mother's school, sought Italian teachers in New York, and then, in the twenties, traveled to Paris to learn from Russian teachers. The Littlefield sisters began to perform and choreograph about the same time as did the

Christensen brothers, and the Littlefield Ballet, begun in 1935, was the first ballet company made up entirely of Americans. The Littlefields, like the Christensens, were leaders in blending the European influences into an eventually integrated American dancing style.

———————

In the teens, most ballet in the world became Russian after highly trained dancers and teachers from the Russian Imperial Ballet schools began to travel outside Russia about 1910. Diaghilev's Ballets Russes and Anna Pavlova's company were only the most famous among the numerous touring bands of dancers.

By the end of World War I, the colorful, oriental *look* of Russian ballet had permeated nearly all American formal dance, but its *grasp* of the art's underlying structure had not. "Ballet" to most Americans meant exotic vignettes—in vaudeville shows, in revues and follies on Broadway, and in the first "all-singing, all-talking, all-dancing" musicals to emerge from Hollywood after sound was invented. Lines of girls in toe shoes and feathers inevitably turned up on revue stages and on movie screens. The finest ballet dancing could be seen in the live prologues to movies at New York's Roxy Theater, which had imported the French ballet master Leo Staats to arrange the ballets.

Gradually, Russian dancers on tour began to stay behind in America, and the ones who became outstanding teachers—Andreas Pavley and Serge Oukrainsky in Chicago, Theodore Koslov in Los Angeles, Alexander Kotchetovsky in Houston, Ivan Tarasov, Mikhail Mordkin, Michel Fokine, and Adolph Bolm in New York— put vigor and imagination into a formerly stiff and sometimes amateurish art form. In the period after the Russian Revolution, many of the Russian artists who had traveled so far from home chose exile. Their knowledge and skills thus came to reside in other countries: the present-day national ballets of England and France, as well as ballet in America, grew from Russian methods and the Russian classical heritage grafted onto those countries' theater traditions and national characters.

Though the seeds of ballet had been sown around America by 1930, the decisive event that would send the spearhead of the art to our shores was the death of Diaghilev in 1929 and the dissolution of his Ballets Russes. Those events left Diaghilev's artist-collaborators bereft in Europe—the dancers along with the sculptors, painters, scenarists, costumers, composers, and choreographers. New organizations arose, and factions seceded from these. One such faction, led by young George Balanchine and Boris Kochno, Diaghilev's former "aide-de-camp," produced, in 1933, a season of ballets in Paris called Les Ballets 1933.

This season was to be significant for the birth of American ballet as we know it now, for the mysterious and wholly modern aura of these ballets seized the imagination of a young American of twenty-five named Lincoln Kirstein. It was Balanchine and his company alone, Kirstein decided, who were carrying on Diaghilev's bold and deft Paris experiments—not the other groups who called themselves the Russian Ballet.

Kirstein, although he had spent summers in London and Paris absorbing high culture and the Ballets Russes, was a true young American of the twenties; he refused to be a mere camp follower of the new company, hoping instead that this avant-garde and now vagrant Franco-Russian ballet would settle in his own country. Kirstein had dreamed of a balletic art that could be American in style and classic-Russian in derivation. One of the first Americans to be passionate about the Russian ballet, he came to understand the time and immense effort required to make a ballet dancer, and the resulting keenness of theatrical expression thus in that creature's power. The Christensens, isolated in Utah, had earlier grasped the whole process of ballet education, and so had the Littlefields in Philadelphia—but as yet they didn't know about the existence of a person with ideas like Kirstein's, nor he about them.

Where the Christensens were doers of the art, Lincoln Kirstein was a born connoisseur from the Eastern establishment, a thinker and a theorist. He shared the longing of many of America's educated intellectuals of the twenties to revive Europe's culture and its traditions in this country—as if in answer to some vacuum of ornament here. It was a longing paradoxically accompanied by an admiration for whatever was truly new and modern in the arts. Kirstein seemed to share such peculiar American divisions of feeling as that, for instance, which impelled an American poet like T. S. Eliot to move simultaneously "backward" into a conversion to the high church of England and forward into new forms and structures of modern poetry. No wonder Lincoln Kirstein was devoted to the Russian ballet, the art that embodied both a rich tradition and a spirit of bold, witty, and even shocking experimentation. And of all the Ballets Russes choreographers, Balanchine, almost as young as Kirstein himself, seemed the most effortless in his blending of very modern effects with very classical ones. Some of Balanchine's works for Les Ballets 1933 were set to traditional Tchaikovsky, Schubert, or Beethoven scores, others to avant-garde music of Kurt Weill or Igor Stravinsky; in them he melded classical steps handed down from the Renaissance with the flagrantly vernacular gestures and behavior of the Jazz Age. Already in the twenties, in his *Prodigal Son*, his *Apollo*, and the other ballets he created for Diaghilev, Balanchine, rather than simply laying intricate modern ideas, costumes, or scenarios on top of old steps, had begun expanding the very ballet vocabulary he had absorbed from his own traditional training.

In 1933, Balanchine and Kirstein began to talk about bringing ballet to America. They found they both believed, for completely different reasons, that any ballet company must be founded on a strong classical school—Balanchine because he himself had been trained in the world's best one, the Maryinsky of Imperial Russia, and Kirstein because he foresaw the utter lack of comprehension in America, even among dancers, of ballet's traditions. Respected schools of the other arts now existed in America. Why not a ballet school too?

Balanchine, Kirstein, and Edward Warburg's (he was a friend of Kirstein's from college) School of American Ballet, which opened its doors in 1934, was the first of a new kind of ballet institution in this country. Instead of a single teacher with his or her name on the door, this was an academy with a faculty that represented several points of view, but only one style—that of the Russian Imperial Ballet school of the Maryinsky Theatre in St. Petersburg (now Leningrad). Balanchine had asked Pierre Vladimiroff, a former soloist of the Maryinsky and of Diaghilev's company, to come teach with him, and shortly thereafter he also asked Muriel Stuart, an English-born protégée of Anna Pavlova and former soloist in her company. Gradually, more Russians joined the faculty of the School of American Ballet (also known as SAB), including one of the greatest teachers America has ever known, Anatole Oboukhoff.

If the teaching of this enterprise was Russian, the first season of the new American Ballet, which began at New York's Adelphi Theater on March 1, 1935, presented *American* dancers in ballets tailored for the New World. Some of these were altered versions of Les Ballets 1933; others were new-made by Balanchine for this country—notably *Alma Mater*, a satire on twenties college life, and *Serenade*, a lyrical ballet blanc.

Serenade, which is still active in the repertory of the New York City Ballet, must have been deeply exciting to those who could "read" it in 1935. With a corps de ballet recruited from everywhere and got ready in a year, Balanchine showed what could be said to American audiences by means of this poetic language of movement, and he went about it in a disarming fashion. He choreographed into the dance some of the uncertainty of those first rehearsals: a dancer who came in late and searched for her place in the pattern, another dancer who tripped and swooned on an exit—these

George Balanchine with School of American Ballet students Chris d'Amboise and Judy Fugate on the set of Don Quixote, *in 1965.*

moments became part of the fabric of the dance. In the midst of this informality, Balanchine evoked the classic ballets blancs of the nineteenth century — *Giselle* and *Swan Lake*, with their ghostly corps de ballet who materialize in a forest. Yet Balanchine's girls made a new kind of corps de ballet: they moved big, like Isadora Duncan and the American "free-dancers." Their long tulle skirts billowing, the female *Serenade* dancers skipped and swooped to the Tchaikovsky music, and were lofted and displayed by the two male dancers who came into their world like the heroes of the old story ballets.

Serenade was especially made by Balanchine *for* American audiences. It was also *about* Americans, about their learning of the style and the mysteriousness of an Old World that wasn't yet theirs, but might become so. It was a graduation ballet. Balanchine's dancers were graduating, as was all of America, into a new cultural amalgam, a New World urban glamour. The quality showed up in other kinds of American entertainment too: the movie musicals of Fred Astaire and Ginger Rogers, the songs and shows of Jerome Kern, Irving Berlin, Rodgers and Hart, Cole Porter. In the thirties, America was consolidating its contribution to the twentieth century: a modern-vernacular mode that had come first out of Ragtime and Jazz and gone into Swing. The mode brought forth a new array of manners—fresh, disarming, unpredictable; Balanchine saw this and put it into many of his American ballets.

The excitement of the new American Ballet company was also, in part, its timeliness. It drew dancers from obscure places, dancers who were mysteriously ready and waiting for an American company. William Dollar from St. Louis had learned ballet from pictures in books while working in his father's store; Eugene Loring, an amateur actor in a Wisconsin little-theater group, had taken up dancing as a hobby; both showed up in New York shortly before Balanchine. The Christensen brothers were gathered in from vaudeville, where they had been appearing with partners all over the country as "The Mascagno Four, Dancers Extraordinaire" (they were doing ballet, of course, but American vaudeville audiences wouldn't yet buy that billing). Many of the girls in the first American Ballet were taken from Caroline Littlefield's school in Philadelphia, because the Littlefield daughters, Dorothie and Catherine, had met Balanchine in Paris when they went there to study.

The new company fought to stay alive. For a short while it became the ballet company of the Metropolitan Opera, but Balanchine's new versions of opera ballets disturbed the patrons. In 1938, Balanchine was won away by Broadway and the movies, and choreographed several classic musicals of the late thirties: *On Your Toes*, *Babes in Arms*, *I Married an Angel*, *The Boys from Syracuse*, and, on film, *The Gold-*

Mimi Paul, Nicholas Magallanes, and Allegra Kent in a 1965 performance of the New York City Ballet's production of Serenade, *choreographed by Balanchine with music by Tchaikovsky.*

wyn Follies. Kirstein proposed to the remaining dancers of the American Ballet that they all "organize some ballets and perform someplace"—and thus was born Ballet Caravan, a touring ballet company that crisscrossed the United States in the late thirties and generated some new, lighthearted American ballets including *Billy the Kid, Filling Station, City Portrait, Show Piece,* and *The Great American Goof.* "The only thing we could dance were the dances we could make," recalled Lew Christensen—and these dances reflected the enthusiastic pride all the company members took in this newly Americanized ballet. The Christensens burned their vaudeville costumes so they wouldn't be tempted to go back on the circuits, but they put vaudeville humor and speed into the new ballets. And why not? Wasn't this fast, active, slightly goofy comedic genre America's own—in movies, in musicals, now in real ballets? Why not use gangsters and mechanics and cowboys as the heroes of ballets?

The army took gangsters, mechanics, cowboys—and American dancers—to fight in World War II, which ended Ballet Caravan. But as the war died down, there was Lincoln Kirstein, himself in the army, eagerly brewing plans for a new company that emerged in 1946 as Ballet Society, "a non-profit members' corporation for encouraging the lyric theater." Its significance lay in its reuniting of Balanchine and Kirstein, and its combining of the Russo–Franco–American repertory of Balanchine with the new rough-and-ready idioms of Ballet Caravan.

After two years of bitter struggle to stay on its feet, the performing wing of Ballet Society was invited in 1948 to be the official ballet company of the New York City Center of Music and Drama; it was renamed the New York City Ballet and, in Kirstein's words, "the future was open."

Meanwhile, the Kirstein–Balanchine combination of companies was by no means the only ballet in America: two other companies were far better known to most people in this country because they lived by touring—the Ballet Russe de Monte Carlo, and Ballet Theatre, which later became American Ballet Theatre. (Diaghilev's company used the plural form, Ballets Russes. References in this report to Ballet Russe denote the Ballet Russe de Monte Carlo, which, during its complicated history, underwent several changes of name, management, and personnel.)

The Ballet Russe, composed of most of the elements of Diaghilev's former company, was first brought to America in 1933 by impresario Sol Hurok, toured to packed houses all through the thirties, and ended up belonging more or less to this country after it was cut off from Europe by World War II. A collection of bravura, sparkling performers—dancers like the Russian ballerina Alexandra Danilova and the Russian-trained Englishman Frederic Franklin—with a repertory of exotic vignettes and elegant, frothy "champagne" ballets, it toured endlessly with full orchestra. When the Ballet Russe came to town, it was like an elegant version of the circus. This ballet was popular for its very divergence from home-town life: these weren't just people, they were dancers from exotic places; even the young American dancers who had joined the company often went by Russianized names.

During World War II, a sudden love of ballet came over Americans. It was something people at home could spend their money on; it was a world of colorful, musical, exhilarating sensations far from the battlefronts and the war news. The Ballet Russe de Monte Carlo basked in the warmth of this public support, and so did the newest ballet company, founded in 1940 with its own concept of what an American style should be. Out of the remains of the company started by Mikhail Mordkin, a former partner of Anna Pavlova, emerged Ballet Theatre in 1939. The new company, it was known in private, was partially supported by the family fortune of one of its principal dancers, Lucia Chase. Its aim was to be not just American but a major company, so it could act "as a gallery of the dance," showing "the masterpieces of all artistic eras and countries and the potential masterpieces of the future." If the United States was where ballet had ended up, went the reasoning, then *all* of ballet should end up here.

To the founders of Ballet Theatre, the idea of a strong choreographer–artistic director promised only trouble. Witness, they said, the artistic stranglehold that Leonide Massine maintained on the Ballet Russe de Monte Carlo, or that Mikhail Mordkin had kept on his company. They hoped that by eliminating a sole artistic point of view they could unite the talents of many artists—choreographers, composers, designers, dancers—much as the old Ballets Russes had done under Diaghilev.

But Ballet Theatre, even as it employed outstanding young American dancers and American choreographers—Agnes de Mille, Jerome Robbins, Michael Kidd, Catherine Littlefield—seemed to owe an allegiance to early Russian ballet too, through its Mordkin origins and its association with Diaghilev's first choreographer, Michel Fokine, who auditioned and rehearsed its first corps de ballet. And in the heat of the wartime enthusiasm for the familiar-exotic, Ballet Theatre was mistaken for a little Ballet Russe de Monte Carlo, put under the management of Sol Hurok, and billed as "the best in Russian ballet." Its Americanness having dissipated during the war years, it emerged as a touring operation almost like the Ballet Russe.

Willam Christensen leading a theater-ballet class at the University of Utah in Salt Lake City.

Meanwhile, just about the time the first Hurok-sponsored Ballet Russe company, on the one hand, and Balanchine, on the other, were arriving in New York, the art of ballet gained a stronghold in the Far West, when the oldest Christensen brother, Willam, decided to return to his home region and teach. Christensen established himself in Portland, Oregon, where modern dance was the prevailing mode, and set up a school to convert students to ballet. In 1937 Christensen traveled south with some of his students to dance for the San Francisco Opera Ballet (then under the control of Adolph Bolm) and in 1938 he became its director.

It is ironic that while the semi-Russianized ballet companies on the East Coast were pushing ballet language toward international-modernist or neo-American folk modes, an American in San Francisco, Christensen, was painstakingly reconstructing ballet's Russian past. No American audience had seen either the full-length classical works of French ballet transmitted via the great Russian schools of the nineteenth century or the Russian works of that time—only pieces of them, like Anna Pavlova's *Coppélia* or the latter-day Ballet Russe's Black Swan pas de deux from *Swan Lake.* Naturally, no record of the complete works was available to Christensen (intelligible records of dancing are a rare commodity); neither were the orchestral scores, since there were as yet no music archives in the West.

San Francisco, though, harbored a big community of Russian émigrés and *they* wanted to see the old ballets. So Christensen went to them for memories and advice.

"The Russians," he said, "would tell me; I would get the score [by ordering Russian music from Europe]; I watched Russian teachers, I read everything—I thought I was searching for a dream." By unceasing imaginative efforts, Christensen managed to produce America's first full-length *Coppélia* in 1939, *Swan Lake* in 1940, and *Nutcracker* in 1944. (The Littlefield Ballet had already mounted a full-length *Sleeping Beauty* in 1935.)

By the end of World War II, the San Francisco Ballet was the largest company in the country; it commanded a handful of major soloists (among them Markova, Dolin, Toumanova, Petroff) and a corps de ballet some forty strong. But it floundered in the postwar years because no one in it knew exactly how to manage a ballet company that stayed in one place instead of touring everywhere, nor how to persuade the citizens of San Francisco to donate money to their ballet just as they donated money to their symphony and their opera.

In 1951, Willam Christensen moved to Salt Lake City because of his wife's health, and the youngest Christensen, Lew, veteran of Ballet Caravan and the School of American Ballet, took over in San Francisco. Gradually, by mounting his own ballets and those of Balanchine, Lew Christensen brought the company to a new strength.

An American Ballet Theatre production of Rodeo, *by Aaron Copland with choreography by Agnes de Mille.*

By the late fifties, the art was flourishing in this country, and it was clear that American dance would make its mark on history. The only question was, which American dance? Which of the companies pointed the way to the future? The Ballet Russe, even with its alien theatrical glamour, was increasingly peopled with Americans; it had even acquired some American ballets, starting with the irreverent and charming *Rodeo* by choreographer Agnes de Mille, hired as a gamble in 1942. Ballet Theatre, despite occasional Russian billings, retained its young American connotations and its "gallery of the dance," including the still-fresh works of the forties in the American idiom. The San Francisco Ballet was building its repertory of both classic and Western-flavored works. And when thinking about dance and America, one had to note that the original kind, modern dance, was ending one of its flush periods; such great Martha Graham dance-dramas as *Letter to the World* (1941) and *Appalachian Spring* (1945) surely provided a definition of American bodies portraying essential American rhythms.

To a casual observer, the New York City Ballet seemed the only dance organization whose claim to Americanness was questionable, since its major choreographer was a Russian and his sources were thoroughly eclectic. Balanchine used French,

Italian, Russian, and American music both old and new for his dances, and he cheerfully scrambled old dance idioms and new ones. Prominent among his works were a martial-patriotic *Stars and Stripes*, to Sousa (1958), an abstract-moderne *Agon*, to Stravinsky (1957), and a classical-romantic Bizet *Symphony in C* (1948; originally *Le Palais de Crystal*) with lines of girls posed in white tutus. No genre predominated. Nevertheless, it was Ballet Society and its performing wing, the New York City Ballet, that the Ford Foundation chose as its partner in its first philanthropic efforts to strengthen dance as an American art. Lew Christensen's San Francisco Ballet was the second partner.

The Foundation believed that to define American ballet by the Americanness of its look was to narrow its possibilities. By the fifties, folk and Western ballets tended to look like a cliché of twenty years before. Not even Martha Graham in the fifties was making "Americana" dances anymore but rather "universal" ones: Greek tragedies like *Night Journey* (1947) and lyric hymns like her dance essay on Joan of Arc, *Seraphic Dialogue* (1955). To look for "American flavor" in dancing was to look for an anachronism. It was past time for a broader, nonpartisan look at dance in this country.

Ted Kivitt and Eleanor d'Antuano in a 1971 American Ballet Theatre production of La Bayadère. *The ballet, choreographed by Marius Petipa with music by Leon Minkus, was first performed in 1877 at the Maryinsky Theatre in St. Petersburg.*

The Program

The Ford Foundation resolved to examine the process of ballet training as well as the connection of training to professional performing. What happened to dancers when they were ready to go on stage? Were there enough companies for them? If not, how to create the kinds of performing outlets that the training implies? Dance companies ranged in scale from the New York companies like New York City Ballet, operating in a smaller space than it wished to occupy, to the touring companies like Ballet Theatre, lacking any home base, to the regional companies struggling to rise above provincial quality.

To begin action, the Foundation decided to commission Ballet Society to conduct a survey exploring just which teachers in the country maintained professional standards and how those teachers could benefit from some kind of network, no matter how loose, that would connect them to a wider world of ballet. Perhaps the appearance in the late fifties in Paris, London, and New York of the great Soviet companies, the Bolshoi and the Kirov ballets—the first Russian national companies to be seen in the West—also called attention to the chaotic condition of ballet teaching in the United States. That modern Russia could draw on a network of twenty-two state-supported schools throughout the Soviet Union, schools fed by a truly formidable recruiting system operating in Russian schools, youth clubs, and community centers, underlined the fact that any ballet company, if it intended to grow and stabilize itself, must depend on a major school that could recruit in a wide territory. This was even more urgently true in this country, where professional attitudes about ballet were not necessarily rewarded with any public notice or financial advantages.

Findings of the Survey

The Ballet Society survey, coordinated by the director of the School of American Ballet, Eugénie Ouroussow, produced in 1962 a clear and vigorous document setting forth the conditions of ballet and ballet training in America. Lively reports were likewise generated by Lew Christensen as he visited schools and auditioned possible scholarship students for the San Francisco Ballet school throughout the West. But long before these documents had emerged, extensive consultation by the Foundation with ballet teachers and civic ballet leaders in every region began to produce a picture of what was going on "out there" in the name of ballet.

The number of so-called ballet schools was astonishing, and so was the number of children taking lessons. Most visible first of all were the strong teachers who had built up their schools and formed companies to serve regions larger than their cities. Josephine Schwartz in Cleveland and Dorothy Alexander in Atlanta, for example, had schools and companies that could be called "regional," while a number of cities boasted what were called "civic" ballet companies inhabiting smaller spheres. But what about the scores of schools not so visible? Distinguishing among all of them throughout the country was the difficult part of the task. To Balanchine, who saw students at two regional ballet festivals in the early sixties, it seemed that every little girl in America was dancing: "It is almost as if they cannot live without the ballet," he said. Why had ballet suddenly become so popular?

For one thing, the fifties had been a decade of child-rearing, of settling down in home towns and suburbs to bring up the children born in the post–World War II baby boom. And where there are children, there are lessons. Ballet was a prime subject of lessons for girl-children in thousands of residential communities in America. Its image spoke of Ballet Russe's fading glamour, the quaint mysteries of the new English Royal Ballet, names from afar: Pavlova, Danilova, Margot Fonteyn. Hollywood had picked up and transmitted the high-gloss, high-class, thoroughly artificial but somehow still-pure aura of ballet in a succession of forties and fifties movies: *Waterloo Bridge* (1940), *Specter of the Rose* (1946), *The Unfinished Dance* (1947), *An American in Paris* (1951), *Limelight* (1952), *Invitation to the Dance* (1957); the greatest of all such films came from London: *The Red Shoes* (1948). Movie ballerinas, though in their films they were often doomed, still embodied the well-bred qualities middle-class America wanted in its daughters.

There was also the fact of geometric progression: the first Russian teachers in America, starting in the teens and twenties, had produced a crop of students some of whom became teachers, and these teachers produced more teachers and more students. Besides these, professionals of the Ballets Russes were gradually retiring and opening up new studios of their own in the hinterland. A whole string of ballet *couples*, men and women dancers who were married—the Roman Jasinskis in Tulsa and the Robert Lindgrens in Phoenix, for instance—taught ballet in different regions and served as a corrective to the notion that ballet was effeminate.

By the fifties, every sizable town boasted or condoned three, five, sometimes ten ballet schools, often in fierce competition with each other. (For instance, Balanchine and his ballerina Diana Adams visited eleven schools in Buffalo in June 1961.) Many of the companies attached to dance studios were growing, and many civic ballets

The Red Shoes *(1948), starring three principals of the Sadler's Wells Ballet—Robert Helpmann* (left), *Moira Shearer, and Leonide Massine—did much to popularize ballet.*

were banding together in regional associations. A National Association for Regional Ballet, for nonprofit amateur companies, came into being in 1963. The idea of "amateur" ballet was a phenomenon unique to America, since the state-supported schools in Russia and other European countries not only supported the students' studios but set professional standards of training. American ballet schools, on their own in a market economy, were forced to be commercial. Few American schools could afford to refuse untalented students and concentrate only on those who showed enough promise to become professionals. Moreover, the children's ingenuous enthusiasm was sometimes swallowed up in their families' desires to see them grow graceful and demure above all else. It was unclear, in this democratic social system, why a teacher should favor some students over others; the nature of dancing talent was obscure even to the parents of children who had it. Professional dancers did emerge out of this system, but chance played a large part in their emergence, and the question kept imposing itself of how much waste of really talented students occurred in such a hit-or-miss procedure.

Some "ballet" teachers had been teaching other kinds of dance, tap or jazz or acrobatic, and had simply added ballet to their curriculum because it was now the thing to offer. Sometimes they taught all different kinds of dance in the same class: fifteen minutes of each style, not forgetting some work on the toes. But the content of the lessons was finally not so crucial as the teacher's approach. One teacher in a Southern city, who taught ballet along with "pantomime and a certain amount of acting and ballroom," struck her School of American Ballet visitors as "a delightful fat lady who has a wonderful way with children"—she would put on records and let them waltz or lightly run around. Yet she, reasoned the observers, "is probably more fruitful and less harmful than the 'serious' ballet teachers who are often misinformed and pretentious." Bad ballet teaching could be dangerous to the young bodies of the students. In the midst of this free-for-all, only a few serious teachers could be found, teachers who understood the logic in the art, the rigorous yet delicate training necessary to mobilize the muscles and bones of the human body into an ingenious machine to jump and balance and reach in lyrical, elastic positions. Sometimes they were discovered when their students turned up at regional festivals, dancing correctly and with flair. "Who was your teacher?" the visitor from SAB would ask; she would write down the address of the school and go there.

First Actions: Regional Scholarships and Teachers' Seminars

The survey produced two immediate actions: the Regional Scholarships and the Teachers' Seminars. The scholarships were designed to bring a small group of talented students, drawn from regional schools, to be "finished" at either the School of American Ballet in New York or the San Francisco Ballet School. In 1960, fifteen young dancers were awarded money to study at the School of American Ballet for the year 1960–61, while eight or nine were brought on scholarships to the San Francisco Ballet School. And in 1961 Balanchine began teaching two-week summer workshops to teachers from around the country, a response to the eager questions about teaching methods that had greeted him in the ballet schools he had visited.

That the first pilot program proved the utility of scholarships of this kind is shown by the success of two of its recipients, Cynthia Gregory of American Ballet Theatre and Suzanne Farrell of the New York City Ballet—two of the finest American ballerinas of our time.

Without the scholarships, these dancers might never have reached the professional stage; they might simply have settled down somewhere and begun to teach. Roberta Sue Ficker of Cincinnati might have become a ballet teacher in Ohio if there hadn't been a scholarship program. Instead, she and her mother and two older sisters packed all their belongings in a station wagon, left Cincinnati, and drove to New York because an opportunity developed for Roberta Sue to study at the School of American Ballet on a scholarship. The mysterious part of the story is how that

young girl, Roberta Sue Ficker, now Suzanne Farrell, already possessed the musical and imaginative talents needed for ballet, and the drive to transcend her provincial training and go on to be the great artist she is now. The fortunate part of the story is that the scholarship existed.

The scholarship students, now under close observation, revealed what problems most plagued ballet training outside of New York. Even if well-trained, they lacked stamina. Many of them had been "rescued" by the scholarships from the constant performing they were required to do as stars of their small regional companies—performing that would have harmed them before too long. The problem involved more than the ability or inability of their original teachers. The financial pressure of running a ballet school prevented teachers from guiding their students to the peak of their abilities—even if the teachers knew how to do so. If the teachers didn't know, there was usually no one they could ask for advice or fresh teaching material.

The other arm of the 1960 action, the Teachers' Seminars, aimed to improve these conditions *and* create an informal network of communication between the School of American Ballet and ballet schools around the country. The twenty-four teachers who spent one week that June attending Balanchine's daily two-hour sessions were stimulated and even disturbed by the intensity of the experience. (Some of them had some trouble executing the exercises they usually taught.) But for most of them the effect of these seminars was to shed new light on an everyday process. The age-

Nineteen-year-old Suzanne Farrell leaps during a 1964 class at the School of American Ballet.

old litany of ballet exercises that had accumulated through the contributions of "great dancers, ballet masters, musicians and costumers" was now being expanded once again. In this and the summer seminars that followed in the next eight years, ballet exercises were taken apart and examined in both anatomic and poetic terms; the rhythms of the exercises were discussed, the color and texture of each exercise were revealed, and the whole dynamic of the art was restated—the dynamic of a new style of ballet fit for here and now. These seminars are preserved only in careful notes kept by some of the teachers who came to them. But the work of the seminars —work amplified in hundreds of classrooms across the country—represents a major contemporary vision of ballet style, one more in a body of visionary contributions dating from the first Renaissance treatise on the art.

This crucial connection between the School of American Ballet and its parent company, the New York City Ballet, exemplified the vital and necessary connection in dance between teacher and choreographer, between the training of dancers and the look of the dances created on them. This holistic view of ballet became the primary principle in the Ford Foundation's larger plan of action for the dance field, which was put into operation in 1963.

The 1963 Ballet Program
With the benefit of nearly five years of information gathering about ballet in America, the Ford Foundation announced on December 16, 1963, a $7,756,000 program "to strengthen professional ballet in the United States." Money would go to both the training and the performance facets of ballet. One-and-a-half-million dollars was set aside to improve teaching in local communities all over the country through scholarships awarded to dance students, the funds to be administered by the School of American Ballet under the general direction of Balanchine. The School of American Ballet itself received approximately two-and-a-half-million dollars over a ten-year period to enable it to become a model institution and a finishing school for scholarship students recruited from places other than New York. The funds for ballet companies were given in various portions to the New York City Ballet and the San Francisco Ballet, and also to five other young companies around the country that aspired to professional standards of performance and that were linked to schools for training dancers. In other words, the grant action attempted to centralize training resources, while at the same time decentralizing professional activity by creating outlets for trained dancers in alternate strong locations outside of New York. Three of the five were new companies: the Pennsylvania Ballet in Philadelphia, the

Boston Ballet, and the Houston Ballet (though it was in its training stages). Two, Frederic Franklin's National Ballet in Washington, D.C., and Willam Christensen's Utah Ballet (later Ballet West), already existed.

But the Foundation's program for dance didn't merely designate seven companies to receive funds; it also embodied a plan for nourishing and in the end perhaps stabilizing the whole pattern of dance training in this country.

Though the plan supported dance training in many ways, the Local and Regional Scholarships program was a separate entity within it that must be looked at alone, since it has arguably influenced American ballet more than any other part of the plan.

At first it seemed nearly impossible to find a way to improve instruction in local communities, given the competition for economic survival among ballet schools in them. What would be the basis for choosing the schools that received support? The Ford Foundation's approach, carefully devised so as not to settle sudden sums on what seemed to be favorite schools but still somehow to support the good ones, was to give the money to the students. This system would be administered not by the Foundation but by a ballet school, the School of American Ballet.

Here is how the Local Scholarships worked: each year during the ten years of the scholarship program, several dancers or teachers from the School of American Ballet traveled from city to city and observed classes in as many studios as possible (in 1963–64, for instance, ninety-one schools in twenty-four states were visited by SAB representatives). From these classes they chose certain advanced students aged anywhere from nine to seventeen—the ones who seemed talented and diligent enough to become professionals. The kids remained where they were, living with their parents, going to their home-town academic schools, and taking ballet with their local ballet teachers—only now, thanks to the scholarships, they could afford to take the number of classes a week they needed—and their teachers could afford to give them that many. What the Foundation intended was not simply to pick up the fees of the lessons but to motivate the teachers to teach more classes.

The Regional Scholarships that followed Local ones created a national structure of ballet training that served simultaneously as a recruiting system for SAB and for the school of the San Francisco Ballet. Regional Scholarships brought the most talented of the Local Scholarship students to study at the summer session of the School of American Ballet, and enabled the most talented of the summer students to remain for the winter term at SAB. This system got the students out of their communities for part of the year, and into a classroom with their peers and with a variety of teachers, but avoided too-great resemblance to the Russian recruiting system, in which

With the help of Madame Sophie Pourmel, a young School of American Ballet dancer dons her costume for a role in a 1974 City Ballet production of The Nutcracker.

the institution took over the life of the young ballet student. Career choices at every step of the way were still left to the students and their parents.

The whole scholarship program reflected the rudimentary truths about ballet and ballet training: the fact that stamina, extensions, pointe technique, ballon (the ability to jump high), and musical instincts must all be trained into any young dancer with aspirations to a dancing career, and that without these the dancer was not trained. Through the SAB-directed network, parents and students could get hold of information to help them formulate a sense of right teaching versus wrong. A ballet school that had conquered its community through flashy recitals instead of through serious and thorough teaching could find nothing in common with the SAB–Ford Foundation scholarship network—and its students couldn't qualify for scholarships. On the other hand, a new or young teacher could get into the network by producing proof of dedication in the form of a well-trained student. In this way professional standards in teaching were given national recognition, which in turn gave interested parents and teachers some criteria for evaluating their local ballet schools.

Over the ten years of the Local and Regional Scholarships program, 127 schools participated in it; 712 local awards were granted; 317 summer-course scholarships to SAB and 138 school-year scholarships were granted. Ninety-four students from the Local Scholarships program found professional employment.

Two other functions of the Local Scholarship program also allowed commercial studios some extra breathing space in their operations: the Beginners' Groups and the Guest Teachers program.

Beginners' Groups gave the teachers a chance to go out of their studios and recruit new students, aged eight to ten, and teach them without fee (that is, at Ford Foundation expense). The idea was to give children from diverse backgrounds a chance at ballet; also to put new blood into the whole art by recruiting youngsters who weren't suburban white middle-class girls—urban black boys, for instance. Under the Beginners' Group plan some teachers—the Roman Jasinskis of Tulsa, Oklahoma, for instance, and the Rozann-Zimmerman school in Chatsworth, California—started special classes just for boys. Other teachers recruited minority children; several Beginners' Groups of Mexican Americans formed in California—as did another of Pueblo Indians in the Southwest, and several of black dancers in Virginia and Washington, D.C.

Under the Guest Teachers program, a local school could request a guest teacher from the School of American Ballet for a period of one to six weeks. It turned out that the demand for teachers always exceeded the supply, but whenever one was available the injection of energy, the fresh perspective on ballet, and the chance for a hard-working local teacher to watch his students in someone else's class were invaluable aids.

Even as funds were reaching local studios through these scholarships, money was also granted the School of American Ballet to hire more faculty, upgrade its administrative staff, increase its scholarships to both regional and New York students, and generally to concentrate more on those students gifted enough to become professionals.

Thus the plan set in motion by the grant of 1963 covered all levels of training from the recruiting of beginners to the "finishing" of the most advanced students in New York and San Francisco. This was the first time that all steps along the way to becoming a dancer had been identified and examined, with support offered at the weak links. It should also be noted that grants to the Pennsylvania Ballet, the San Francisco Ballet, and the National and Houston ballets supported the independent training schools and informal recruiting systems of these institutions.

Many observers doubt that, without such a thorough experiment and without one dominant influence trying to create a consistency in one wing of ballet training from beginning to end, anything would have happened to change the ballet scene in the country for a long time. Teaching in each community would have remained just as uneven, and few studios outside of New York would have had access to training resources like those of the School of American Ballet and the San Francisco Ballet. Even so, the country still produces too many young dancers who are trained, flexible, precise, but completely colorless—since no awareness of ballet exercises as live material for a choreographer or a performance has been given them. The difficulty in teaching ballet is that the style must be taught through the steps, in order that the student may understand what is supposed to take place not only with the mind or body but with the whole being.

Apart from assistance for training in local schools, most of the help given to companies in the 1963 grant action included aid to their schools, their scholarship and recruiting programs, and their company apprentice programs; in other words, to whole systems of training and performance. This is because in ballet, more than in any other art, training doesn't end with school but goes right on into the company. Even the most famous dancers, the top soloists, take at least one ballet "lesson" or class every day; it is their regular practice, their work on their instrument. A choreographer playing on that instrument can sometimes "teach" the dancer far more than he or she has learned in years of classes.

Only the New York City Ballet and its school, the School of American Ballet, despite their association, were given separate grants in the program of 1963, because these institutions had developed more distinct identities than corresponding institutions in other parts of the country, even to having separate administrations for school and company operations. Moreover, the School of American Ballet was now mobilizing to undertake massive new activity, as it organized and conducted the Local Scholarship program already described.

The New York City Ballet

One should note that the growth of the New York City Ballet over those years when the Local Scholarship program was in operation enhanced this program immeasurably. Gradually, as students were brought to the School of American Ballet on scholarship, and as some of them entered the New York City Ballet, that company itself became much more of a national company, with a corps de ballet filled with young people from California, Texas, and Ohio, as well as from New York City.

But if "new blood" from around the country changed the tone of the company and gave new ideas to Balanchine, Jerome Robbins, and other New York City Ballet choreographers, there is a sense in which, with Ford Foundation aid, the New York City Ballet, by the early sixties already the most substantial American company, simply continued along its self-appointed course. (Between its first performances in 1948 in City Center and its selection by the Ford Foundation as the major grant recipient in 1963, the company had premiered an astonishing eighty-seven ballets.) Ford Foundation money simply gave it a wider scale of operations and enabled it to better regulate its finances.

By the end of the first year of the grant to NYCB, salaries for administrators and artistic personnel had been put on a more just basis; the staff were no longer helping to subsidize the ballet out of their own pockets; a costume shop had been created, partly to preserve traditional costume-making skills; and seven new productions had been mounted.

But the intention of the Foundation and City Ballet from the beginning was not only to flesh out the company on the inside but also to involve its dancers in activities outside New York City. Money was used for subsidizing company performances away from home, lending soloists at less than the usual fees to smaller companies, and filming some of the repertory so it could be preserved and eventually seen by other than New York audiences. In short, given the nature of dance as a nonrecordable, nonpackageable, live performing art, this was an attempt to expose audiences, as well as teachers and potential dancers, to a company that had been practically invisible to them.

By 1973, the end of the first decade of Ford support for the New York City Ballet, the company had grown to eighty-three members, and its repertory had been increased by seventy-one new ballets. It had made appearances at arts festivals far from Manhattan and had completed four European tours. Its management and financial practices had been steadily solidified.

In 1964 the New York City Ballet moved into fresh quarters at the New York State Theater at Lincoln Center, and in 1966 it began its association with the Saratoga Performing Arts Center, founded on the site of the old spa of Saratoga Springs, New York—an outdoor summer theater where orchestras, drama groups, rock stars, concert musicians, and others would perform. The New York City Ballet was invited to be the resident ballet company in the first year of SPAC's operation. For the last sixteen years, the company has performed there for three- or four-week seasons, and recently they have sold out most performances.

The School of American Ballet followed its parent company into new quarters in August 1969, moving from a two-studio space above a café on upper Broadway to four studios in the new Juilliard School at Lincoln Center. Besides the studios, Juilliard also provided modern locker rooms, offices, faculty lounges, and a feeling of spaciousness.

Lew Christensen in his 1938 Ballet Caravan production of Filling Station, *with music by Virgil Thomson and book by Lincoln Kirstein.*

The San Francisco Ballet

In the late fifties, the San Francisco Ballet under Lew Christensen was still a small company that gave a regular season of only two weeks a year in San Francisco; three months of the year it was attached to the San Francisco Opera. By 1959, the company had accumulated twenty-three company dancers and six principals whom Christensen had trained, the nucleus of a dance troupe with large possibilities. Balanchine especially admired his training of male dancers, some of whom, like Conrad Ludlow, had already joined City Ballet.

When the Ford Foundation awarded the San Francisco ballet and school a grant in the 1963 program, Christensen laid out a plan of expansion that included spending more money on the institution (on its administration, for example), enlarging the scholarship program, increasing the professionalism of the company, and extending its performing season. The company immediately added one-and-a-half administrative positions, two ballet teachers, and two pianists and set up a workshop and lecture demonstration program to give young dancers who were in the crucial transition phase between school and company some professional onstage experience. In 1965 the San Francisco Ballet School acquired two of the most outstanding Russian ballet teachers in America, Anatole Vilzak and his wife, Ludmila Shollar, both of whom had been trained in the Maryinsky School and had danced leading roles in the Maryinsky Theatre and in Diaghilev's company.

The company had already acquired the material of a unique repertory, starting with Willam Christensen's productions of the classic story-ballets, continuing with Lew Christensen's own ballets—the lively ones from Ballet Caravan days, like *Filling Station*, and the humorous-classical ones from later, *The Dryad, Jinxed, Con Amore*—and adding a new full-length *Nutcracker* and a *Beauty and the Beast* to a Tchaikovsky score. Over the years, through both the company and the school workshop, the San Francisco Ballet has tried to develop new choreographers out of its own ranks, and has succeeded to a degree remarkable among the major companies.

Aid to Newer Companies
National Ballet
Pennsylvania Ballet
Ballet West
Houston Ballet
Boston Ballet

The 1963 grant action attempted to lay a base of support for other professional companies and schools beyond the already established New York City Ballet and San Francisco Ballet, in the hope that these other companies could grow up to be strong new centers of ballet and perhaps in time create clear styles that were like neither the New York nor the San Francisco style. These five companies were chosen for reasons consistent with the other parts of the grant: they had fine schools. Each company had come about through the vision of an artistic director who was also a major ballet teacher and thinker within the art form.

It is interesting to ask how each of these communities—Washington, D.C., Philadelphia, Salt Lake City, Houston, and Boston—came to have a ballet company even before the Ford Foundation appeared on the horizon. The answer involves the people in these cities who started the companies. In Philadelphia, Salt Lake City, and Boston it was a dynamic ballet teacher who was determined to have a company and who, little by little, accumulated a board of local citizens to help. But in Washington and Houston it was a nonballet person or people who started the drive for a ballet company, who went out, found an artistic director, and invited him or her to set up shop.

Curiously, the two outright failures among the grantee companies of 1963 were the ones whose artistic directors were not originally connected to that community. No one could have predicted this in 1963, since to any casual observer the five new companies seemed to represent the full range of origins and backgrounds, all equally legitimate, that made up American ballet. The Utah Ballet, soon to be Ballet West, was another Christensen enterprise, begun out of the ballet department at the University of Utah that Willam Christensen had started when he left San Francisco. The Pennsylvania Ballet and the Boston Ballet were two companies founded by Americans who "came home" to teach ballet: Barbara Weisberger, a Pennsylvanian, had studied in New York but began teaching in Wilkes-Barre, Pennsylvania, then moved to Philadelphia; Virginia Williams of Boston had actually never left New England but picked up bits and pieces of information and fused these into an extraordinary comprehension of the nature of ballet. The Houston Ballet and the National Ballet in Washington were the companies directed by foreigners: in Houston a Franco-Russian ballerina, Tatiana Semenova, was invited by an ad hoc group of Houston citizens to head the small company that would become the Houston Ballet; an Englishman, Frederic Franklin, former soloist and ballet master of the touring Ballet Russe, landed in Washington and assumed command of that city's ballet.

Houston had a special relation to ballet. For years, that city was the traditional stopover of the touring Ballet Russe at Christmas, the city where the company's tired dancers could stay put for two weeks of performing while celebrating the holiday with hospitable Texans. The dancers loved Houston and the Houstonians loved ballet—but a glamorous Russian-style ballet; this is why Houston picked one of ballet's aristocrats to create their company. Madame Semenova had been trained by the great Mathilda Kchessinska in Paris, taken on by Balanchine there in his 1933 season, and then featured for years in the Ballet Russe and the Paris Opéra Ballet. She was a thorough, strict teacher and a choreographer, before the Ford grant, of several ballet divertissements. But it is possible that her legendary experiences slowed her up. She refused to put untrained dancers on the stage, but she couldn't train them fast enough to suit board members truly hungry for their own ballet. When, in 1967, the Houston board replaced Semenova, they contravened one of the conditions in the grant and thereby caused the Foundation to discontinue its funding. The Houston board faltered and then rallied to pursue its plans, with remarkable dedication.

Not long after, in 1973, a third, more stable version of the Houston Ballet received a substantial Ford Foundation grant.

The original Washington, D.C., attempt lasted longer than the first Houston one. Franklin, by 1973, was directing a sizable troupe and had built up a solid traditional repertory that emphasized choreographic classics more than any American company of that time. By contrast, however, the school seemed an afterthought. Founded only months before the company, the school was what the board was willing to sacrifice when matters got tight. Then, when a lag appeared in the matching-fund schedules of the Ford grants, the National Ballet's major organizer and patron, Mrs. Jean Riddell, stepped in and generously made up the difference. Unfortunately, her very generosity made it unnecessary for other Washingtonians to form a loyalty to their ballet. So, without a fund-raising base, the company finally disbanded in 1973, two years after the Foundation had awarded it a second grant.

––––––––––––

The failure of the Washington company, unlike that of the one in Houston, was largely financial. It was understood by the Ford Foundation from the beginning of its activities in the fifties that dance companies were then at a crucial point in their overall histories, because constant touring, the habit of both Ballet Russe and Ballet Theatre, had worn itself out as a means to "keep" a ballet company. Production costs were rising and so were the salaries of stagehands, musicians, and occasionally dancers—everyone, that is, who contributes to producing an evening of ballet in the theater. No general economic strategies had taken the place of touring, yet it would not do to deprive the whole country of professional ballet because the old formulas didn't work. The way to find new ones seemed to lie in attaching a dance company firmly to a home base and then building an organization around it by means of modern techniques of financial management. No longer could one very wealthy person or family sustain a whole dance company into the future, given inflation and the spiraling costs of producing ballets. Rather, all the board members of a company must do it, and they must be deeply committed people, knowledgeable in business and interested in raising endowments, employing investment experts, regulating cash flow, building subscription audiences, and developing fund-raising plans. There was a recognition in the Foundation that more emphasis had to be placed on the managerial side of ballet companies. From the start, each new company faced gigantic financial and operational problems, both foreseen and unforeseen, since the very thought of serious local ballet was absolutely new to middle-class

Americans, who had only relatively recently grown used to supporting serious symphonies, museums, and opera companies in their home towns.

These were the questions the Ford Foundation tackled in its awards to the six non–New York companies, awards that covered anywhere from five to ten years and that included stipulations for matching funds to be raised by the boards of the companies. In a sense, all the new companies were pilot projects and therefore financial gambles. But the Foundation had decided in 1963, because there were no secure ballet *institutions*, to put its money on the people behind them.

The Boston Ballet and Philadelphia's Pennsylvania Ballet were two of the more successful ventures of the 1963 grant action. The initial troubles of these two companies came from the old money in those cities—not a feature of Houston or even of Washington. When the ballet came on the scene in Boston and Philadelphia, it had to beg: Bostonians and Philadelphians supported symphonies, operas, and museums—familiar cultural institutions—but ballet was new to them. The attractions of dance were not yet felt in these cities; the rich and powerful there did not flock to the boards of ballet companies, nor had there yet appeared publicists and administrators who could drum up the requisite excitement. Following the 1963 grants, the Ford Foundation gave a series of further grants to both the Boston and the Philadelphia companies in an attempt to build the management skills and the fund-raising power these companies needed to become permanent institutions. Organizational and financial know-how was offered as well to the two original artistic directors of the Boston and Pennsylvania ballets.

The strength of commitment of these two artistic directors was the secret weapon of both companies. Boston's was E. Virginia Williams, a New England woman who had grown up with old-fashioned free-form "aesthetic" dance. She had always believed, as had Moes Christensen, that there must be a kind of dancing *like* ballet, and she eventually found it. When she opened her first school in the mid-thirties, she bribed students wanting "tap and acrobatic" to take ballet lessons, by offering the latter free. These classes, soon full, were taught soundly and imaginatively, since Williams had made it her business to find out from every possible source what constitutes good ballet teaching. Soon she was running two studios, one in the city and one in the suburbs, and taking troops of ballet kids to New York on weekends for further training from the finest Russian masters. She herself spent many hours in private sessions with Balanchine before he began his Teachers' Seminars.

As for repertory, the lively spirit that has always gathered about Boston Ballet's

A 1981 Boston Ballet production of Tchai-kovsky's Swan Lake, *with Marie-Christine Mouis and Donn Edwards.*

repertory probably came from Virginia Williams's own personal revelations about ballet. Since ballet history had been unknown to Americans for so long, perhaps there was a special excitement in the early sixties about gathering a selection of works that would reveal ballet's past to present-day audiences and perhaps, if one were lucky, say something about ballet's future. The Pennsylvania Ballet's initial repertory also suited the spirit of an enterprise for which there was no previous model. In fact, all the new companies outside New York were naturally involved in creating new "galleries of the dance," each one different from the others. The Boston Ballet had mounted a number of Balanchine's dances in its repertory, reconstructed a good range of ballets from the past, and made a point of presenting new dances, both modern and ballet, by young unknown choreographers. In 1967, Williams entered the universal search for new choreographic talent by inaugurating a nation-wide annual choreography competition. The Boston Ballet is also a company that has encouraged its own dancers to create works for the repertory, recognizing that the finest choreographers of the past have come from within the apparatus of a company, where a dancer or ballet master can know the dancers—his or her material—thoroughly and instinctively.

Although the Pennsylvania Ballet encountered the same conservative patterns of philanthropy in its city as had the Boston Ballet, it became a model company in the period following the Foundation's dance grants of 1963. Its founder, Barbara Weisberger, had already been director of a regional ballet company in Wilkes-Barre, Pennsylvania, and of a ballet school in Philadelphia. Since Weisberger had danced with the Littlefields of Philadelphia, it was logical for her to come to that city and begin the first small performances of a company formed from within her school, which she did a year before there was any assurance of Ford Foundation support for ballet. Not only one of the best American-trained teachers of her generation, Weisberger was also a person gifted with organizational talents and a grasp of what the nuts and bolts of a local ballet company might be, at a time when no one knew much about that.

From the beginning, Weisberger, like directors of other newer ballet companies, attempted nothing less than a company that would be at the same national level as the New York City Ballet or Ballet Theatre. And she tried it not by featuring famous guest stars but by building a strong school and then a young ensemble, outfitting it with good learning ballets from the classical repertory and the Balanchine oeuvre, and not forgetting to offer her audience its own world premieres. Weisberger shares the belief of most dance directors that a contemporary ballet company exists as material for choreographers, something very different from a museum of dancing. She therefore adopted a courageous policy about her repertory, emphasizing new, often experimental works—a policy with a high risk of failure built in. The scarcity of sound, new choreographers has been felt not alone by the Pennsylvania Ballet, but by all the ballet companies in America and Europe and the USSR. Strong features of the Pennsylvania Ballet were a coherence of approach to the ensemble dancing in the company and an emphasis on the musicality of the dancing. Weisberger was one of the first artistic directors to hire a musical director to work with her.

Barbara Weisberger instructing a class at the School of the Pennsylvania Ballet.

The ballet company in Salt Lake City was the only company helped by Ford Foundation grants whose base was not a major metropolis. Yet the smallish city, perhaps because of its Mormon character—the Mormons who "went strong for music and dancing"—has stood solidly behind it. As the company grew, it found that even with community support it lacked a broad enough audience or fund-raising base to sustain the kind of ballet company Willam Christensen wanted. He had put together a repertory of his own works, along with brother Lew's and Balanchine's; because of his intelligent teaching, the company performed as one unit of healthy, young, somewhat bravura dancers. The problem of a support base for Ballet West was partially solved in 1969 when the Federation of Rocky Mountain States chose it to be the official ballet company of this thinly populated region. Ballet West paradoxically became a local company with a home base vast enough to make it a touring company as well.

Additional Ballet Companies Added to the 1963 Grant Action Plan
The Joffrey Ballet
The Dance Theater of Harlem
In 1962 and 1963, the Robert Joffrey Ballet, a group of young American dancers performing American works, toured the Near and Middle East, India, Pakistan, and the USSR under the auspices of the U.S. State Department. Robert Joffrey, a dancer and choreographer from Seattle, had started his company in 1954. In 1956, with six dancers and a station wagon, he toured twenty-three cities in eleven states. Until 1962, the Joffrey Ballet had received no outside support whatsoever, but in that year it was adopted by Rebekah Harkness, and was thus already taken care of when Ford decided on its program. Not so a year later, when the young company was dropped by the Rebekah Harkness Foundation and in the process lost half of its dancers and all its records, administrative staff, and repertory to its former patron.

Throughout the early sixties the Ford Foundation had been helping companies that showed a vital and imaginative approach to the question of an American repertory and an American style for a ballet company. The Joffrey Ballet had shown such an awareness, so the Foundation now granted funds to help Robert Joffrey rebuild his company and his repertory. By the end of 1965, the Joffrey Ballet existed again and ten new ballets had been made on it. The Joffrey saw itself as something different: a major young company with a repertory of contemporary American choreographers of modern dance as well as ballet. Besides the grant for start-up expenses, the Joffrey Ballet received regular support for company activities once it was in operation again, and for the company school, begun by Joffrey in 1953 and always an important New York training center. Once it got going again, the Joffrey grew by leaps and bounds: by 1967 its repertory had jumped to twenty-seven ballets from the original ten. In 1968, the company performed at the White House, appeared on the cover of *Time*, and held a workshop in Houston on how to start a ballet company. The Joffrey, like the Pennsylvania and Boston ballets, appeared important to the future of classical ballet in America. All three were repertory companies, not tools for a single choreographer. Yet each of these companies could demonstrate a clear style of dancing, a particular communal awareness while performing, an ensemble identity.

Robert Joffrey's multimedia ballet Astarte, *which premiered in 1967, includes a score by the rock group Crome Syrcus, scenery that moves in counterpoint to the dancers' movements, and projected photography by Gardner Compton.*

In 1968, yet another emerging ballet company offered virtue beyond the character of its repertory, its style, or its school. Originating in Harlem, it was one of the first attempts at a classical ballet company most of whose dancers were black.

The director was Arthur Mitchell, whose own dance career had already broken new ground. Mitchell, a self-taught social dancer, had won a scholarship in modern dance at New York's School of Performing Arts, where he noticed that the strongest dancers were ballet dancers. Mitchell wound up at the School of American Ballet, then joined the New York City Ballet as its first black member. His dancing career continued triumphantly through the sixties, and Balanchine created a number of roles especially for him.

In 1968, Mitchell chose to come home to Harlem, which had no known connection with ballet, in order to give his community what ballet had given him. He began in the Harlem School of the Arts, founded by Dorothy Maynor, a concert soprano who dreamed of a cultural school for Harlem children in Harlem itself, to expose the children to the arts, and to train them on their own territory. Soon, however, Mitchell left Maynor's school and began to concentrate on his own particular mission of an arts conservatory built around a strongly led independent dance component.

He was brilliant at animating a school. In 1971, even though the school was housed temporarily in the basement of a church, it consisted of 123 youngsters on full scholarship and a company of twenty-four dancers in training. Mitchell concentrated at first on lecture demonstrations and school performances, rather than on all-out concerts. And he began to stuff skills into the many children who came to him, in a whole range of classes from sewing, dancing, and music, to costuming and even accounting.

Mitchell believed his school could sustain professional ballet standards even as it

Arthur Mitchell rehearsing members of the Dance Theatre of Harlem, 1970.

provided a vital social force in Harlem. To make it truly available to that community, he set his rates so low that every child got the equivalent of at least a partial scholarship. All the teaching, though, was of professional quality.

By 1971 the school had found new quarters in a Harlem garage purchased with money donated by Mrs. Alva Gimbel, and had expanded to an operation of seventy-five classes weekly, with 1,200 students enrolled for the winter term, rising to 2,000 during the summer months. Mitchell's claim that donating money to his Dance Theater of Harlem was "investing in individuals" had been proved: he was sending children back to their grade schools and high schools with a new pride, not rhetorical but real—physical—won in the work on bodies and minds in ballet class. The dancers in the company, Mitchell made startlingly clear, were expected to be "personal ambassadors of the Dance Theater of Harlem," agents of a new and better image of Harlem. And not only were Mitchell and his staff turning out dancers, they were also training junior producers, lighting technicians, costumers, administrators, and eventually professional musicians. By 1975, DTH had generated the nucleus of its own orchestra.

At the heart of this whirlwind of community activity was DTH, a truly professional organization. In March 1971, the company made its New York debut with a repertory made up partly of works choreographed by Arthur Mitchell and partly of Balanchine ballets. It turned out that the dancers of DTH commanded an elegant performing style of their own, a style that could create a fresh perspective on familiar works. The DTH dancers approached the Balanchine ballets with fearlessness and bravura musicality. Style, in fact, appeared to be uppermost in the minds of Mitchell and ballet master Karel Shook from the start.

Mitchell's company gave American ballet another dimension—an emphatically non-European one. They were the visible proof that a choreographer or architect of a ballet company can choose a model from history and infuse *another* spirit into it, so that he recalls and honors that model but does not repeat it. Black American dancers made what were once Renaissance court gestures into something really contemporary.

After seeing DTH, one reporter for a black newspaper in Oakland, California, confessed that the feeling in the black community before Dance Theater of Harlem appeared was "that the essentially European orientation of classic ballet, with its court traditions and ethnic flavor, is totally remote from black culture. But then," he continued, "I go to see Mitchell's company—and I say to hell with it. This dancing is meaningful to these people and these audiences."

American Ballet Today

The New York City Ballet

In the seventies, the New York City Ballet did things on a grand scale—in the operational sphere as well as in the artistic. In 1972 the company staged a Stravinsky Festival, for which Balanchine, Jerome Robbins (who is also a ballet master of the company), and several other choreographers made twenty new works. Twenty world premieres and ten revivals occurred in a single week, a different program every night. Clive Barnes, writing in *The New York Times*, called the festival a "kind of divine madness"; that divine madness recurred in the spring of 1975 in a Ravel Festival of similar proportions, in 1981 in a grand and splendid Tchaikovsky Festival, and in 1982 in a second Stravinsky Festival. Many of the ballets from these festivals have entered the repertory of the New York City Ballet, a fact that implies a creative machinery operating continuously within the company on a massive scale. The festivals have also served to shower a sort of intense musical education on a willing public: exposure to large portions of a composer's oeuvre, conducted by such a world-class figure as NYCB's principal conductor, Robert Irving, can be had nowhere else in either the music or the dance world. And in between the different festivals, new works were created on the order of Balanchine's *Union Jack* (1976) and *Vienna Waltzes* (1977) and of Jerome Robbins's Verdi ballet, *The Seasons* (1979). In addition, the more recent festivals have served as proving grounds for a New York City Ballet principal-dancer-turned-choreographer, Peter Martins, who has tackled all kinds of music in all sizes of ballets. (Now that Balanchine is dead, Martins, along with Jerome Robbins, leads the company.) The company, meanwhile, is constantly being replenished with young dancers from the School of American Ballet, which now numbers more than one hundred students. A sign of the range of City Ballet—in age, expression, style, training, and background—can be seen when a great mature ballerina like Suzanne Farrell appears in Balanchine's wild "Amazonian" *Walpurgis Nacht* (1980) alongside the meteoric young ballerina Darci Kistler, who, though still a teenager just out of the School of American Ballet, is dancing like nobody else before her.

The School of American Ballet

The Foundation's 1963 action had made it possible for the School of American Ballet to be as selective and supportive of talented needy students as the best of the state ballet academies in Europe. And the Regional Scholarship plan had enabled SAB to establish a genuinely national character. By 1974, however, it was clear to the school's management that SAB could not expect another decade of Foundation support comparable to the decade just past, and that SAB itself must take a more active and systematic role in fund raising for its current and future operations. Early hopes that the Foundation might assist SAB in creating an endowment had to be abandoned. To help SAB through a difficult and crucial period of transition, the Foundation in 1974 approved a grant of $2 million payable over a five-year period.

The School of American Ballet has had an enormous impact on ballet training through the Local Scholarship program that it administers. Teachers now have greatly increased access to developments in the art as a whole, and schools can decrease their reliance on being commercial dance factories. It isn't that the old American-style tap, toe, and personality schools have disappeared—they're out there for the people who want them—but should a school be interested in producing dancers, that school can become part of this informal network, which once revolved around the School of American Ballet's Ford Foundation scholarships and which now includes winter and summer programs at the schools of the Joffrey Ballet, the Pennsylvania Ballet, the Houston Ballet, and the San Francisco Ballet, and in the winter at the University of Utah, along with Ballet West's summer school in Aspen, Colorado. The recruiting and scholarship system originated by SAB and the Ford Foundation has been adopted by each of these companies to one degree or another. All, however, recognize that wider recruiting and more careful attention to finishing students is the only way to achieve future growth.

The Local Scholarship program ended formally in 1972, complying with the original agreement of ten years earlier when the money was granted. In the final year a team of five experts in the dance field traveled around the country visiting schools active in the scholarship program, to see what had gone on. The evaluators, who knew the eccentricities of ballet training in this country, were pleased to discover that teaching standards had risen nearly everywhere. The scholarship program had apparently benefited the teachers in ways far beyond the financial.

American Ballet Theatre
Up to the early seventies, all the dance companies aided by the Ford Foundation maintained strong artistic direction and firm attachment to a home base. Ballet Theatre, since 1956 American Ballet Theatre, represented another conception of a ballet company: it toured frequently, it was co-directed (from 1945, by Lucia Chase

and Oliver Smith); it hosted a variety of choreographers with no single artistic voice predominating. Though American Ballet Theatre, or ABT as it is popularly called, continued to command the services of internationally known soloists and choreographers during the fifties and sixties, the company often operated under severe financial strain, twice having to suspend operations. When the Ford Foundation initiated its major ballet development program in the sixties, ABT's unwillingness to engage in long-range planning and development precluded its involvement in the program.

Nevertheless, by the late sixties, ABT had begun to stress one of the elements in its artistic approach that was important from its beginnings: preservation of the classic nineteenth-century "story ballets." The company's first full-length *Swan Lake*, in 1967, followed by a new production of *Giselle*, in 1968, gave it a strong position in an American ballet community experiencing a new surge of interest in ballet's past. In 1969, a newly elected slate of ABT officers helped the company's management put ABT on a sounder financial basis. By 1972 the company had been strengthened enough to qualify for a $1 million "stabilization" grant under a new program —initially called the Cash Reserve program—developed by the Foundation to improve the balance-sheet positions of performing arts companies.

In the mid-seventies, American culture seemed to wake up again to the virtues of ballet—in fact to the virtues of all kinds of dance, not excluding tap. The media called it the Ballet Boom or the Dance Explosion. Ballet students no longer had to apologize for studying this "anachronistic," "elitist" art form; communities throughout the country saw, as if for the first time, the fascination in this youthfully energetic and extravagantly physical mode of expression. Perhaps the vogue for dancing has something to do with the contemporary preoccupation with fitness; perhaps the totality of a dancer's art brings out a romantic streak in modern audiences. Certainly the seed money planted in the sixties by the Ford Foundation, in regional companies and local ballet schools, touched a great many households. Many dance companies have begun to bask in the glow of the current conviction that dance is perhaps the key art of the twentieth century. But popularity and expansion bring their own difficulties, which, added to the current economy, have caused many arts organizations to put aside various visions and concentrate on the box office.

In this age of growth and consolidation, the main problems confronting dance companies are those of succession, space, and repertory. The only company presently exempt from these conditions is the great NYCB, whose longtime principal choreographer, Balanchine, made the most of its repertory as well as large chunks of other companies' repertories, and who continued until shortly before his death in 1983 to create several new ballets a year. Jerome Robbins, the other senior choreographer at the NYCB and now, as mentioned earlier, its co-leader, has done likewise. And as for space, that problem was first solved in 1948, when the NYCB came to reside at City Center, and solved again in 1965, when Lincoln Center's New York State Theater became its home.

Many of the pioneering people and organizations in American ballet now face the need to introduce a new generation into the decision-making process. But which members of that generation? And how to bring them in? The question of space is also key: dancers who must rehearse various ballets at the same time take up a lot of floor space, and if there is a school involved with the operation even more space is required. It is crucial to the health of a company and a school to have a home: not to have to move pianos and clothing and bulletin boards periodically from one rented place to another. And finally there is the question of repertory, which in a sense is the most challenging of all: how is a company to decide which ballets it will present? Will it invite new choreographers? Will it try to make choreographers out of its own ballet masters and dancers? Will it revive ballets from the past? And which past: the Russian, the French, the American? A company's repertory of ballets is really what proclaims its identity to the public as well as to the world of dance. The competition is intense for finding ballets that haven't been done before, ballets that say something fresh about a company's capabilities or its habits of thought, and yet can still offer the dancers a clear challenge to their technical and performance skills. The past few years have been a time of great change for American dance companies, whose various responses to the problems of control, space, and repertory provide a fascinating panorama of the state of the art.

In September 1980, Mikhail Baryshnikov took over the directorship of ABT from Lucia Chase and Oliver Smith. Audiences at ABT have since seen the corps de ballet infused with a new spirit along with many new members; they have seen corps dancers brought up through the ranks to perform as demi-soloists or soloists. In 1981, ABT moved both its administrative offices and its rehearsal studios to new quarters, at 890 Broadway—the first time that ABT's offices and studios were brought together under one roof. ABT also hopes to strengthen its scholarship program for promising dance students and to strengthen its second company, now named ABT II, the smaller, more mobile group that gives young dancers valuable stage experience. Baryshnikov retains the same sort of repertory as his predecessors—one that is strong in forties Americana and in the nineteenth-century French and Russian classics. Being Russian, Baryshnikov will undoubtedly maintain a solid showing of old and new full-length classic ballets (a grandiose *Cinderella* is in preparation for 1984). But besides the old works and the classics, the repertory has recently seen the healthy addition of such diverse items as two early Balanchine ballets, *Bourrée Fantasque* and *Symphonie Concertante*, and an ensemble work, *Duets*, by the arch-Druid of the modern-dance avant-garde, Merce Cunningham.

In 1982, the Ford Foundation approved a further stabilization grant to ABT of $150,000.

The Joffrey Ballet

Robert Joffrey has always shared the artistic directorship of his company with its choreographer, Gerald Arpino, who turns out a steady stream of contemporary ballets. In the seventies and early eighties, the Joffrey's non-Arpino repertory has been one of the most interesting and unpredictable in ballet: it is known not only for its highly "with-it" pieces, such as Joffrey's rock ballet *Astarte* in 1967, and Twyla Tharp's *Deuce Coupe* in 1973, but also for its unusual revivals—Kurt Jooss's twenties work *The Green Table* in 1967, and the spate of early Diaghilev re-creations starting with *Parade* in 1973.

The Dance Theatre of Harlem performing Balanchine's Allegro Brillante, *with music by Tchaikovsky.*

After many years as resident company at the City Center, which meant regular New York seasons supplemented with yearly tours across the country, the Joffrey Ballet in June 1982 accepted the invitation of the Music Center of Los Angeles to become a resident company of that city. The Joffrey's training company, the Joffrey II Dancers, which tours extensively, will remain in New York, as will the company's school. The Joffrey thus will be resident, in effect, in two cities, even as it continues its habit of performing in other large American cities. But within a year or two, most of the Joffrey's playing weeks probably will take place in Southern California locations.

Dance Theater of Harlem

In 1977 most of the Dance Theater of Harlem's top soloists were lured away to commercial theater spots, but in 1979 a new, reconstituted DTH, with a young corps de ballet drawn from the DTH school, carried off a triumphant tenth-anniversary City Center season—"a testament," said one critic, "to the power of the school-company relationship." Since then the company has appeared yearly in New York City at the City Center and presented its customary repertory, in which a number of substantial Balanchine ballets (Mitchell retained close relations with his former

The Feld Ballet's Three Dances, *which premiered in 1983. Eliot Feld choreographed the work with music by John Cage.*

mentor) alternate with DTH's trademark jazz-and-folk-influenced modern ballets, as well as careful, interesting re-creations of ballets from the past. For instance, the jewel of the 1981 DTH City Center season was Michel Fokine's voluptuous Art Nouveau *Schéhérazade* (1910). Only DTH, with a stylishness and theatricality unique among ballet companies, could have pulled this one off. DTH has also toured extensively in Europe, Australia, and the Far East. In the summer of 1981 it became the first black company to appear at the Royal Opera House in London's Covent Garden.

Since its inception, DTH had received substantial funding help from the Ford Foundation. But Arthur Mitchell and the Foundation came to agree that DTH's future could not include operating support from the Ford Foundation indefinitely. In 1976 the Foundation approved a major grant of $1.5 million that provided decreasing operating support over a five-year period, and thus time in which to diversify a base of support for the future.

In the fall of 1981, DTH took what was probably an inevitable step but one crucial to its future: it cut back classes at the DTH school. Instead of the "open door" policy it had maintained up to that time—which meant enrolling, practically free of charge, any student who wanted to study ballet—the school would now be geared to students who showed potential for professional careers. Almost without realizing it, DTH had become a professional school. Besieged by eager ballet students from as far afield as Europe and Hong Kong, it decided that its first responsibility lay with its professional company, and with the kind of training the term "professional" implies. "You see, it's quality we're after," Mitchell explained to *The New York Times.* He has hired for DTH a new managing director, the company's first outside public relations firm, and its first outside costumers and set builders to "dress" his ballets in quality and style.

The Feld Ballet

Eliot Feld's career began in modern dance, where small dance companies composed of strong individuals "speak" the dance language that their artistic directors have created. Yet in 1966, when Feld began to choreograph for ABT, where he was a dancer, he clearly preferred to work with the full range of formal matter—balletic, musical, theatrical—that traditionally constitutes ballet choreography. His first company was the American Ballet Company, founded in 1969, just three years after his first ballet was created. It was a hybrid, with a ballet repertory of works both by Feld and by past choreographers, but it was a small, tight, hand-picked company of

44

individuals, on the order of a modern dance company. His second company, founded in 1973 with help from the Rockefeller Foundation two years after the first one folded, has the same look and feel about it: Feld dancers seem to be chosen for their unique qualities of expression as well as for their technique. It is clear from their performance that they receive some of the best nurturing and coaching available in dance today. The Feld Ballet is noted both for its collective ambition and for its ability.

After several years in which Joseph Papp made the New York Shakespeare Festival's Newman Theatre available to the Feld company, Papp himself decided to occupy it, leaving the Feld Ballet temporarily homeless. Undaunted, the company, with the help of its principal backer, LuEsther Mertz, found and created a handsome rehearsal space with four enormous studios at Broadway and 19th Street. Almost simultaneously it found an old art-movie theater in the same neighborhood, which Mrs. Mertz purchased. After $4 million in renovations, the Elgin Theater has been reborn as the Joyce Theater, New York's "brand new, elegant, and intimate 474-seat" space, to watch small- and middle-sized modern dance and ballet companies—a kind of theater that New York sorely needed. Other companies will perform in the Joyce, but the Feld company opened there, after an absence from New York of three years, in 1981, in a lavish five-week season that featured ten Feld ballets, five of them New York premieres. Feld has always been skilled at creating a diversity of moods in his ballets, and locating those moods in the music, costumes, sets, and lighting. Especially striking were his evocation of Depression America in *Scenes* and his picture of urban punk violence in *Over the Pavements* (both 1981).

The Feld organization also operates the New Ballet School, which recruits disadvantaged minority-group children and offers them a chance to study dance seriously. The Ford Foundation's stabilization grant to the Feld Ballet is aimed at helping both school and company keep fiscal affairs on a steady course.

Companies Outside New York

San Francisco Ballet
Houston Ballet
Pennsylvania Ballet
Boston Ballet
Ballet West
North Carolina Dance Theatre

Over the years, American regional ballet companies have faced crises and setbacks, "bumping their heads," says E. Virginia Williams, "on many immovable objects." A number of them have turned out to be vibrant organizations with their economic naïveté left behind forever. The country is in fact now rich in ballet companies: besides those assisted by the Ford Foundation, there are also fine, healthy ballet companies in Atlanta, Cleveland, Columbus, Cincinnati, Pittsburgh, Oakland, and elsewhere.

Today the San Francisco Ballet appears to be one of the healthiest of these non-New York companies. Since 1962, when it took into its ranks nearly all of the first Ford Foundation scholarship students, the San Francisco company has continued to do most of its recruiting in its own school. That means that its tradition of building from inside the organization stretches farther back than any American company's other than the New York City Ballet.

And it's not only an ensemble that is being built there, but choreographic power as well. The crucial step was taken in 1973, when Lew Christensen gave half of the directorship of the company to a much younger choreographer, Michael Smuin, one of his own San Francisco dancers, who had been away dancing and choreographing for Ballet Theatre. Smuin has since made a hefty portion of the company's repertory. His super-theatrical works, including the full-length *Romeo and Juliet* (1976) and *The Tempest* (1980), have attracted enormous attention. The opposite condition from most ballet companies holds here: young talent at the San Francisco always gets a try at choreographing. Three other members of the company, assistant director Robert Gladstein and two dancers, John McFall and Tomm Rudd, have been producing new ballets for the past few years. This is the company that has done most to realize the American ballet concept—which was born in the example of Balanchine and the NYCB—of choreography as the ultimate product of a ballet company—of choreography and dancers being created at the same time.

In 1976, after the overhaul of its administration, the San Francisco Ballet received a Ford Foundation stabilization grant of nearly one million dollars. About the same time, the school of the San Francisco Ballet was put on a stronger footing, with an organized and finely graded curriculum taught by a staff of young ex-professional dancers. The company performs in the San Francisco War Memorial Opera House an average of sixteen weeks a year, and it tours most of the remaining time. (A June 1980 tour of Latin America was a great success.) After many years of consolidating, the San Francisco Ballet commands the resources needed by a healthy professional dance company in America today: its own academy, ample rehearsal space, an apprentice group, a young corps de ballet drawn from its school, several choreographers within the company, and its founding artistic director actively working with his younger, chosen successor.

In the summer of 1976 the Houston Ballet, after several years of searching, invited the English-born former ballet master of the London Festival Ballet, Ben Stevenson, to become its artistic director. Since that time Houston has been a whirlwind of ballet activity. Stevenson has seen to the creation of a full-scale academy, in a made-over warehouse in Houston's suburbs, and the academy, run on the principles of English ballet training (the Royal Academy of Dancing's teaching code), has begun feeding apprentices and corps members into the company. Meanwhile, Stevenson set about mounting full productions of the classics—*Swan Lake*, *Sleeping Beauty*, *Cinderella*, and, most recently, *Peer Gynt*—as well as shorter ballets created by him and by the internationally known choreographers he has invited there. In 1981 the Houston Ballet made a successful debut in New York, and in the spring of 1982 it completed a successful tour of twelve European cities. At the International Ballet Competition held in Jackson, Mississippi, in 1982, the Houston dancers, along with Stevenson, won five medals.

The Pennsylvania Ballet, through 1981, enjoyed widespread critical acclaim as one of the most professional ensembles outside of New York. But by 1978 its artistic momentum and the scale of its performances throughout the United States had propelled the company beyond its fiscal limitations and very nearly beyond the control of its board and management. Over the next three years, despite the rich and varied repertoire on stage, the company resorted to a series of fiscal and organizational expedients that undermined both its professional objectives and its artistic leadership. The company's two artistic directors—founder Barbara Weisberger and Benjamin Harkarvy, an American ballet master who had previously worked at the Dutch National Ballet—resigned in 1982. In July of that year Robert Weiss, a principal dancer with the New York City Ballet, was named artistic director.

The Boston Ballet has found a more harmonious way to begin to share artistic control of the company. Joining E. Virginia Williams, the founder and director of the company and the school, is Violette Verdy, the professional dancer and teacher best known in this country for her years as a principal in the New York City Ballet. The Boston Ballet school, although not yet fully streamlined with an apprentice system connecting it to the company, continues to contribute dancers to its parent company,

Members of the Houston Ballet in Élégie. *The ballet, with music by Stravinsky, was choreographed by Balanchine for the Ballet Society and premiered in 1948 at the City Center of Music and Drama.*

47

Ballet West performing the 1980 ballet Brahms/Haydn Variations, *choreographed by Daniel Levans.*

as well as to other companies outside of Boston. The Boston Ballet regularly performs in the old, vast, but newly renovated Music Hall, now renamed the Metropolitan Center. Boston's centerpiece production of 1981, planned to match the scale of the Metropolitan Center, was also a tribute to the team spirit within the artistic management. It was a semi-traditional *Swan Lake*, whose first and third acts were created by the company choreographer, Bruce Wells, its second act by the ballet master, James Capp, and its fourth act by co-artistic director Verdy. The whole was brought together with set and costume design created by the world-famous English artist Julia Trevelyan Oman. This approach shows how unconventional a "regional" company can be, and how it can contribute to the still young but already richly varied culture of American ballet.

Ballet West also brought in, in 1976, a young artistic director, Bruce Marks, to work with its longtime head, Willam Christensen. Marks came most recently from American Ballet Theatre and the Royal Danish Ballet, with his wife, the Danish ballerina Toni Lander, now Ballet West's principal teacher. The company benefits from its connection with Willam Christensen's dance department at the University of Utah, which draws young dancers with the triple promise of good ballet training, possible connection to a professional company, and a university degree. Under Marks, the company explores the work of new modern dance choreographers, as well as the traditional ballets and training methods of the great nineteenth-century Danish choreographer August Bournonville.

The North Carolina Dance Theatre was founded in 1970 by Robert Lindgren, a teacher and former soloist with the New York City Ballet. Originally the company was an affiliate of the North Carolina School of the Arts in Winston-Salem. In addition to serving the cultural interests of North Carolina and the Appalachian re-

gion, the company was formed to provide experience and jobs for graduates of the school.

Students in an American Dance Festival class at Duke University, 1982.

Eight years later, North Carolina had become a professional company of sixteen dancers, with a reputation of artistic achievement and fiscal responsibility. It has toured widely—as far afield as Kansas, Texas, and the Dakotas. Soon after it became an independent organization in 1978, it was awarded a stabilization grant from the Foundation. Its repertory consists of the works of such established choreographers as Balanchine, Tudor, and Ailey, as well as developing newcomers.

With strong schools at Ballet West, North Carolina, San Francisco, Pennsylvania, Houston, Boston, and other cities, as well as in New York, there appears to be a confusion of training centers. Which one should a student choose for the summer, which for the winter? Where will he face the stiffest competition? Is such intense competition good for him? Perhaps this period of sorting out teaching styles and recruiting territories is a necessary transition to the further strengthening of schools and companies in the regions, and to better, clearer school-to-company connections. A return to the random state of affairs in ballet that occasionally and miraculously produced great dancers must not be permitted to occur. Today's great dancers, very good dancers, and their teachers, choreographers, and board members have struggled too long to reach this point to allow that to happen.

49

Right: *Twyla Tharp, whom dance critic Arlene Croce has called "the Nijinska of our time."* Below left: *the legendary Martha Graham in the title role of her 1960 ballet* Alcestis. Below right: *Paul Taylor (at right)* *and his company in his 1966 ballet* Orbs, *with music of Beethoven.*

Modern Dance

Though it did not provide direct continuing operating support to modern dance companies, the Ford Foundation awarded several grants in the sixties that tried to help some modern dance companies perform on major stages and build broader support systems for themselves.

In 1968, responding to a growing audience for modern dance and the demonstrable connection between these dancers and avant-garde artists, musicians, and theater directors, the Foundation gave a series of grants to performing-arts entrepreneurs who planned to put on a total of twenty-five weeks of modern dance in three theaters around New York City in the fall of 1968 and the spring of 1969 (City Center, the Brooklyn Academy of Music, the Billy Rose Theater). The Foundation assumed one-third of the costs of the project; the rest was provided by the National Endowment for the Arts, the New York State Council on the Arts, and other foundations. Similar efforts to develop audiences for modern dance were attempted elsewhere. And, in 1979, after it had begun to support modern dance companies directly, the Foundation allocated $120,000 for a cooperative marketing effort involving five major modern dance companies: Alvin Ailey, Merce Cunningham, José Limón, Murray Louis, and Alwin Nikolais. The idea was that by pooling audience development and promotion costs, the amount a single company ordinarily would have spent for marketing costs—typically fifty cents for every dollar earned—could be reduced by at least half.

Inner-city children training at the Alvin Ailey Dance Center, 1982.

Alvin Ailey Dance Theater and the Major Moderns

The first substantial grant to a single modern dance company was to the Alvin Ailey Dance Theater in 1974. The Ailey company was an anomaly: instead of serving as a vehicle for one choreographer, as did most modern dance companies, it functioned as a repertory company of predominantly black dancers who performed in a broad range of dance styles. The Ailey company was closer in format to a repertory ballet company like the Joffrey than to other modern dance companies like Merce Cunningham's or Martha Graham's. A school was also connected to the company, offering classes in many techniques, ballet, modern, and jazz. The Foundation's grant was one of the stabilization series to dance companies and academies; it combined the standard elements and conditions of the stabilization program, but included

Right: *Laura Dean performing in the Brooklyn Academy of Music's NEXT WAVE series.* Below: *Merce Cunningham (lower left) and company in his* Quartet, *which premiered in 1982. A former soloist with the Martha Graham company, Cunningham studied dance at the School of American Ballet.*

supplementary funds for scholarships and subsistence stipends for talented and disadvantaged students at the Ailey school. The Ailey company set a precedent for other modern dance companies, after it realized in 1972 that in order to remain a viable and healthy institution with a future it would have to reorganize its company, school, and board on a new financial basis. That was why it came to Ford for help.

By 1978, several other modern dance companies had come to the Foundation for help and advice. In 1978, the Foundation made stabilization grants to four "major moderns," the companies of Merce Cunningham, Alwin Nikolais, Murray Louis, and Paul Taylor, followed in 1979 by a grant to Twyla Tharp's company.

In addition to the major modern dance companies, the Foundation assisted two organizations that had been pioneers in the modern dance field. In 1968, it gave a grant to the Martha Graham company to film some of the Graham repertory. The dances chosen were *Seraphic Dialogue* (based on the life of Joan of Arc), the satirical comedy *Acrobats of God*, and *Cortege of Eagles* (dealing with the legend of Hecuba and the fall of Troy).

Since the thirties, the American Dance Festival has been a school for modern dance students and a showcase for modern dance companies and individual choreographic styles. The young modern dance rebels of the twenties—Martha Graham, Doris Humphrey, and Charles Weidman, among others—all participated in the early summer-long festivals as teachers and commissioned choreographers. Their descendants—both the ones who carried on their convictions and the ones who rebelled against them—continue to form the main body of the festival's faculty. The festival provides a living history of modern dance with all its passionate factions; it serves as a showcase for established companies and for such newer ones as Laura Dean's and Charles Moulton's. It moved in the late forties from its Bennington College base to Connecticut College. Then, in 1978, it was invited to settle at Duke University. The move to North Carolina, which the Foundation assisted, gave the festival's director, Charles Reinhart, a chance to add even more performances and training programs to the festival's activities. In 1980 the Foundation gave the festival a grant of $150,000 to help it attain a healthier financial footing while a civic committee set about meeting the festival's current and long-range funding needs.

Left: *The Nikolais Dance Theatre in the 1964 work* Sanctum. *Alwin Nikolais, who began his professional career as a musician, studied dance with Hanya Holm and Martha Graham.* Below: *The Murray Louis Dance Company in the 1982 work* A Stravinsky Montage.

Postlude

For some ten years, beginning in 1963, the Ford Foundation was the major single source of funding for dance in America. The companies it helped served as catalysts for the surge of interest in dance, an interest demonstrated by the rise in the annual audience for live performance from one million people to seventeen million in just fifteen years, plus an untold number who watch dance on television. Dance in the United States has become an art form of enormous appeal, one that captures, in movement to music, an energy and a beauty that people everywhere can appreciate. Its growth over the past twenty years has made it a more important part of the life of American cities, towns, and suburbs than was ever imagined when the Ford Foundation first stepped into the field.

W. McNeil "Mac" Lowry joined the Ford Foundation in 1953, became director of the Foundation's Humanities and the Arts program in 1957 and vice president for humanities and the arts in 1964. During more than twenty years with the Foundation—he retired in 1975 —he was the principal architect of the Foundation's dance program.

Interviews

INTERVIEW WITH W. McNEIL LOWRY

ELIZABETH KENDALL: Had you always been interested in ballet?

W. McNEIL LOWRY: My personal observation of ballet began, really, when I came to New York to join the Ford Foundation in 1953—four years before the Foundation's program in the humanities and the arts was created. I would often go to see ballets at the New York City Center, not because I was anticipating a program in the arts but simply because I wanted to get more experience with dance.

EK: How did the Foundation's program in the humanities and the arts come about?

ML: In 1957, with the assent of the Foundation's president, Henry T. Heald, and vice president William McPeak, I proposed the Humanities and the Arts program, and in talking about the arts I spoke of the creative and performing arts, lumping under "creative arts" literature, musical composition, painting, sculpture, and choreography. What I wanted to do was to get organized philanthropy, for the first time, into a systematic gathering of information about the arts from the artists themselves and into objectives about the arts that had to do with the values underlying them.

The initial exploratory program had a budget of only $2 million, and if I never got permission for a larger program, if after five years the Board of Trustees wanted to cut it out, that was fine with me. I still thought that enabling a foundation staff to be knowledgeable about artists, directors, managers, and even patrons of the arts, just as they were knowledgeable about educators and scholars and specialists in other fields, was important.

EK: In what way was this a departure from the past?

ML: The Foundation had been involved in a number of arts-related fields, but only tangentially. The few things that had been done in the arts—like Robert Saudek's *Omnibus* series with Alistair Cooke—had been regarded by the Foundation as a means to other ends, particularly in international cultural relations.

What the arts lacked at that time was a national program, national attention from outside that was in any way organized and that expressed any personality or conscious objectives. It was those objectives that I wanted to try to articulate, with a very small staff, but with the instrument of the Foundation behind me. Before we entered the field there was not a single institution of any kind equipped to do field work, field investigation, to find out what the arts situation was. In this undertaking I had almost a clear field.

EK: How did you go about that field work?

ML: I *wasn't* doing systematic reading about the arts. In fact, one of the principles I announced to my staff and to the Board of Trustees was that we were not going to *read* about the arts and make ourselves able to explore their problems that way, through books; we were going to get it from the people who were doing it. And not just the directors and leaders and managers and choreographers, but the dancers, actors, painters, and so forth.

President Woodrow Wilson once said that to create a public policy you brought together the person who had the facts and the person in a position to act. I was in a position that staggered me, because I could see that in the institution I was in—the Ford Foundation—to which I had become very devoted professionally in four short years—I could in effect be both the person who had the facts and the person in a position to act upon them.

EK: Once the arts program was approved, what did you do?.

ML: "Got on my horse." My associate program director, Edward F. "Chet" D'Arms, and I visited 175 communities in the first eighteen months, talking to anybody we could find in any of the arts. People asked why we were going all through the Middle West, the South, the Southwest, the Far West, and so forth, and I said, "Because that's where it is." I didn't know what was out there on the highly structured basis one could find in New York City. But whatever was out there was touching people, making them want to professionalize themselves.

EK: How did the people you visited react?

ML: They were first startled and then moved that somebody cared from way off somewhere. When they found that this somebody was from the Ford Foundation they were quite moved, and one of my jobs—which I did assiduously —was to explain to them that the Foundation's program meant nothing to them yet because it was an exploratory, and limited, program that might become no more than that. But the fact that somebody cared and didn't just read his mail and didn't just see the people who came to his office—although I did that too—changed by itself a lot that was going on in the arts.

As for dance, I myself went to hundreds of dance studios around the country, and D'Arms and others went elsewhere. Then I started bringing people in to the Foundation's New York office, individually or in groups. One of the things I thought was that I needed help sorting out some of the dance teachers I'd met, and the help had to come from professionals. (I was no ballet teacher, so I couldn't do it. I knew what I saw, but not what I was looking at.) I also knew that whatever professionals I chose for Foundation support, I couldn't take them all from one place, one school or company, without people feeling that I was going to try to manipulate the art or to puff up one group or one person. So, in addition to George Balanchine of the New York City Ballet, I chose people like Walter Terry and Allan Hughes, and people from American Ballet Theatre, to serve on an advisory committee about dance training. This was not in an effort to put blue ribbons on a certain number of teachers in the country, but rather to try to build the grapevine, to help both teachers and students be more visible.

EK: What was George Balanchine's role in the Foundation's dance program?

ML: In those pre-1957 days, when I was regularly attending performances of the New York City Ballet, I had begun to realize what it was that accounted for the special magic around the name George Balanchine. I had been talking for several years with Mr. Balanchine (as I had with Lincoln Kirstein, Walter Terry, Doris Hering, Diana Adams, and many others) about the dance program when, in 1958 or 1959, Mr. Balanchine took advantage of something I'd been proposing to him for some time: that he go out and look for himself. When he came back from an extensive trip to schools and teachers of dance around the country, he came to see me and announced that we were going to have a ballet company in every state, that he had seen this big brushfire going on that I had been telling him about, seen the young people, seen their enthusiasm. I told him we would *not* have one in every state—where were we going to get the money? From the people, he said. I said that the government was not going to do it, and that even if it were there were not fifty people in the country capable of heading a ballet company—not yet.

But through the ballet seminars he conducted for several years and through his other teaching and advisory efforts, he inspired dance people across the country to strive for excellence, to become capable of heading a ballet company, or of serving as an artistic director, or of being a professional dancer.

EK: What about the educational network that was set up, which was, I think, the most ingenious part of the whole program?

ML: One of the problems with the educational program was the dollar-fifty to three or four dollars a lesson that people paid at all those dance studios. It may not seem like much, but in part as a result ballet was confined largely to middle- or upper-middle-class girls whose parents were willing to pay that amount week after week. And everyone was asking, "Where are the boys?" Even the national companies were asking that, but the problem was particularly acute "out in the territory." In cities, all the dancers were coming from the most affluent enclaves; there were few if any young blacks or Chicanos. The New York City Ballet did include a number of people who started out as poor, dead-end kids, but it didn't work that way in Tulsa or Kansas City or Houston, for example. I wanted to change that.

We were barred legally from giving money directly to schools or companies unless they were nonprofit, and very few of them were. So we had to work through an intermediary, and the one I selected was George Balanchine's School of American Ballet. So that it would not be felt that we were giving Mr. Balanchine too much power over ballet, we said that for every student selected for training by SAB, the ballet schools themselves—those around the country that were providing candidates for advanced training—were to select another and teach him or her for free—that is, at Foundation expense. And they were to be selected in open auditions, not just in the studio but in high schools and so on, and not just students from the "best" neighborhoods.

EK: How, looking back, do you think the whole program worked?

ML: Well, it was right for its time, it was productive, and it changed the whole face of ballet. It kept ballet from remaining an eclectic, disparate group of original civic companies that might—I want to be fair—*might* over time have become something like what we've got now. But I didn't believe so, and I still think it would not have happened without the Ford Foundation.

Interview with Cynthia Gregory

Cynthia Gregory received a Ford Foundation dance scholarship in 1960, joined the San Francisco Ballet in 1961, and American Ballet Theatre in 1965. She is one of ballet's international stars.

ELIZABETH KENDALL: Tell me why you began to study ballet, and about your first teachers.

CYNTHIA GREGORY: I was born in Los Angeles and my parents were both from musical families. My mother loved ballet. So, when I was five years old, they started me taking ballet classes with a woman named Eva Lorraine, in Pasadena. She had what was called the First California Children's Ballet Company, and when I was six or seven years old I was already on point, and on stage.

At eight-and-a-half I went to Carmalita Maracci and Michael Panaieff, he having been with the Ballet Russe. Carmalita had her own small concert group, which had performed at Carnegie Hall and done tours around the United States. She was a flamenco dancer and classical ballerina with an incredible technique in both areas. She was more of an interpretive dancer. Imagery was her thing. She was very inspiring.

EK: When did you realize you were serious about ballet?

CG: When I was twelve or thirteen, I began to study with André Tremain, who had also been in the Ballet Russe and who had the Santa Monica Civic Ballet. He taught me the Black Swan pas de deux from *Swan Lake,* the *Don Quixote* pas de deux, all those major classical pas de deux. I performed in *The Nutcracker* and several other ballets with the Santa Monica Civic Ballet, maybe four times a year. I guess I became more serious at that time.

EK: How did you first learn that some kind of scholarship was available?

CG: When I was thirteen, Jacques D'Amboise and Maria Tallchief, both of the New York City Ballet, came to one of the studios in Los Angeles and were guest teachers there in the summer. It was a huge studio and there were more than a hundred dancers in the class—maybe even two hundred. André Eglevsky taught, too.

One day when D'Amboise was teaching a class he took two of us aside and asked if we wanted to come and take a class with the New York City Ballet that Mr. Balanchine was teaching. We were asked if we wanted a Ford Foundation scholarship to go to New York.

EK: What happened?

CG: I was very excited that Mr. Balanchine had chosen me to come to New York, but my parents didn't want me to leave home when I was so young.

And they couldn't move to New York. So they said thank you, but no.

I was very disappointed, but then I got very interested in my schoolwork and I wanted to stop dancing and be a normal kid. My parents said I could stop my piano lessons but they had spoken to Carmalita about my dancing and she had said, "Don't let her stop completely. Maybe just one class a week can keep her going." I did that for six months.

Then the next summer Jacques D'Amboise came back again. I got more interested in ballet again, and took his classes. In the fall of 1960 the San Francisco Ballet was down in Los Angeles performing with the San Francisco Opera, which they did every year. At a ballet performance I went to, Jacques D'Amboise happened to be there and so was Lew Christensen. Jacques saw me and remembered me from classes and from my not going to New York City Ballet and he said, "How would you like to meet Lew Christensen? They have a Ford Foundation scholarship program in San Francisco."

I got a scholarship. So did another L.A. girl, Nancy Robinson, later with the Joffrey Ballet. I was fourteen and she was a year older. My mother decided to come up to take care of us. So we found a school and an apartment, and on New Year's Eve 1960 we moved. My father came up on the weekends to visit us and finally decided to get a job in San Francisco.

EK: What was the San Francisco Ballet like when you were there?

CG: It was terribly exciting, because I had never been around a professional company before. The dancers were very well trained. Lew Christensen's choreography was diverse: some ballets very much like Balanchine and others more dramatic or comic than Balanchine-style work. Lew Christensen was the main force in the company. Everybody was afraid of him.

EK: Did you dance on stage right away?

CG: I was in the school for about two months, and then they had their spring season and used us—me and the other nine or ten scholarship students—as apprentices. We danced in the *Symphony in C* and a couple of other ballets.

EK: Did you feel like sort of a band apart from the rest of the company?

CG: Yes—and we were. We had special classes. We had to take one or two classes a day after school, and three classes on Saturday.

EK: There must have been some excitement about the fact that you scholarship students were there.

CG: Yes, for us and for them. The company members were good to us. They worked with us.

EK: I believe that when you were still very young you were brought to New York for a day by the Ford Foundation. Tell me about that.

CG: That was August 1961. I remember we stayed at the Barbizon Hotel for Women, and that we had a chaperone. There were about five girls. It was my first trip to New York.

EK: Were you slightly overwhelmed by all that attention?

CG: Yes, we felt very special. There was a luncheon for all the girls in the New York City Ballet scholarship program, and Mr. Balanchine came. They took us to this conference room in the Ford Foundation building and we all sat around the table, and they asked us questions about how we liked it and what the classes were like.

EK: How did you fare in the San Francisco Ballet, and why did you decide to come to New York?

CG: That first year I was still fifteen-and-a-half. In December I was given a chance to do a solo, the Arabian Dance in *The Nutcracker,* with another Ford Foundation student, David Anderson. From that point on they gave me more and more solos to do, I understudied big roles, and I got to do the lead in *Beauty and the Beast* when I was seventeen. I worked with the San Francisco Opera, too, and finally became the ballerina in *Traviata* and *Aida* and all those operas that have ballets. So it was very diversified, which was exciting. You had *The Nutcracker,* you had all of Balanchine's repertoire, Lew Christensen's repertoire, the opera, and so it was a really good company. And from the age of sixteen I was doing one-night-stand tours with the company for eight weeks at a time.

San Francisco was wonderful, but New York was the place to be. Even Lew Christensen and Harold Christensen would go back to New York and visit Balanchine and come back with new ideas from his school. Whether they wanted to or not—and they *didn't* want to—they helped perpetuate the idea that New York is *the* place.

One summer I asked Mr. Balanchine if he would take me into the New York City Ballet and he said he loved my dancing but that he could not as long as I was with Lew and the San Francisco Ballet. He said that if I decided to leave and come to New York, there would be a place for me in the New York City Ballet. And so I started making plans.

About a year later, in April, we came to New York and had a week's season in the New York State Theater. This was right after Ballet Theatre's twenty-fifth anniversary season, so we were in town a little bit early and we went to watch some of Ballet Theatre's performances. I had been planning to come to New York City Ballet, but I saw Ballet Theatre and I just loved their repertoire—it looked exciting and different to me. I made up my mind then that I would try to get into Ballet Theatre instead of New York City Ballet.

EK: Can you be more specific about what really drew you to Ballet Theatre at that time?

CG: I had been brought up on the New York City Ballet, Balanchine, and the San Francisco Ballet, plus the classics from watching the Royal Ballet and that sort of thing. But here was a company that combined in one program *Combat, Les Noces,* and *Miss Julie.* It intrigued me that there was more to ballet than *Sleeping Beauty* or *Swan Lake,* and more than Balanchine's *Serenade* and *Symphony in C*—which I loved.

EK: What do you suppose might have happened had there not been that Ford Foundation scholarship or that Ford network?

CG: Well, perhaps I wouldn't have been a ballerina but would have led a more normal and interesting life! I don't know. I probably would have gone to New York a bit sooner after high school and I may not have gone to San Francisco at all.

EK: What about the way you *did* do it—with a scholarship?

CG: That way gave me a more serious outlook on the dance. It helped me to be around the company. I think it was better to be with the San Francisco Ballet than with the New York City Ballet in a lot of ways, because I had a more well-rounded background there dancing with the opera, doing the workshops, and so on. It was a smaller company. I had more of a chance to do solo roles earlier, and we toured more. When I came to Ballet Theatre I had a much better background and I was more confident.

INTERVIEW WITH SHEILA ROZANN

ELIZABETH KENDALL: How did you first become involved with dancing?

SHEILA ROZANN: As a child in Massachusetts, I studied tap and a little ballet—
really just tap with ballet slippers. My desire was to study "real" dancing,
but I didn't know exactly what I meant until an aunt took me to see *Song
of Norway,* choreographed by George Balanchine and starring Alexandra
Danilova. *That* was the kind of dancing I'd been looking for. After I saw
Song of Norway, I went to study with a teacher who had the most Russian-
sounding name in the telephone book, Bronislava Nijinska. I listened and
learned the craft from her, but my real teacher was Balanchine. Indirectly,
he formed my taste from that first thing of his that I saw.

EK: What was it about *Song of Norway* that so struck you?

SR: It had big jumps, patterns, partner work, and beautiful bodies doing beautiful steps. I had never seen anything like it before. I began to read ballet
books after that and the photographs that appealed to me—showing dancers
with long legs, incredible feet, an uncluttered look, and never seeming to
be posing or "emoting"—always turned out to be photographs of Mr. B's
dancers. But Nijinska's classes were good for me: at least things had names,
and professional dancers came to visit her. And, since this was right after
World War II, the G.I. Bill was in effect and lots of men were in ballet
class.

EK: How did you become a teacher?

SR: I had started studying ballet too late to think of performing. I gave up hope
of that, went to college, and married. But I still loved and thought about
ballet and in 1954 I opened my first school, in Hollywood. I had children
and showgirls in my classes. I never enjoyed working with dancers from
other schools. Even when I first started teaching I had a definite idea of
how I thought dancers should look and move. It had a lot to do with the
line of the body while it was moving, and with underplaying the ego or
personality of the dancer.

EK: Did you find you had a gift for teaching?

SR: Yes. I would put my hands on people and, in a sense, go inside their bodies
so I could feel how they could correct themselves.

EK: How did your school get connected with the School of American Ballet in
New York?

*Sheila Rozann founded the Rozann-
Zimmerman Ballet Center in Chatsworth,
California, and ran it for many years with
her partner, Eleanor Zimmerman. The center,
flanked by an animal hospital, an insurance
company, a music store, and a cocktail lounge,
is in a long, low Sun Belt shopping plaza
within sight of the wrinkled desert mountains
bordering the San Fernando Valley.*

SR: In 1959 I moved the school to the San Fernando Valley; if the children can't come to you, you have to come to them. In 1961 the New York City Ballet performed *The Nutcracker* at the Greek Theater in Los Angeles and auditioned local children. One of my girls was selected, picked by one of Balanchine's principal dancers, Janet Reed. The next year Janet Reed came back, saw the same girl, and said she'd never seen a child make so much progress in one year. Then Mr. Balanchine himself came to see a class, and afterwards he said, "Would you like to come to a Teacher's Seminar?"

EK: Did you go?

SR: Yes, with Eleanor. We went that summer and every year thereafter, whether there was a seminar or not. Mr. Balanchine taught us his idea of what ballet is—down to how the little finger is held. And he communicated by thought as I did; he would touch people where they needed to feel. We learned an incredible amount in those seminars. We went to all of them, and heard things we'd never heard before. Everything he said we tried out on our students after we went home.

EK: What about the Ford scholarship program in your school?

SR: Diana Adams came to hold an audition for scholarships soon after Mr. Balanchine's visit and picked the same child who had been chosen for *The Nutcracker*. Afterwards an SAB scout came every year, and every summer we sent children to study there. [*A former Rozann-Zimmerman scholarship student, Heather Watts, is now a principal dancer in the New York City Ballet.* —EK]

EK: How did the scholarships, both local and regional, affect the school?

SR: We tried to play down the whole idea of these scholarships. At first I was so excited about the kids going to SAB that I almost went with them. But there was *so* much bad feeling in the school, partly as a result of the scholarships, that we became more democratic. We didn't pull kids off the barre and put them first in the center, or things like that. We didn't, in short, ruin the school. Every child in the room had a chance to audition. The visiting SAB representative had to choose the person with no hints from us. If you got a local scholarship you usually had a crack at New York.

EK: How were the scholarships announced to the children?

SR: We always told them before the audition, "No matter what happens at the audition, *our* evaluation of you won't change." And, of course, they had to learn how to take an audition. But the SAB people almost always chose the ones we wanted them to. We've become stricter over the years. Now we don't let children go to the auditions just because they have a good ballet body or good feet. We look to see if they have the right temperament and the fortitude to be a dancer at the level of SAB.

EK: How did the scholarship program affect you personally?

SR: It helped me to feel part of the real world of ballet. It helped our status with parents. It gave the children confidence.

Over the years I've grown bolder. In the first two years of training we usually don't keep the children who present discipline problems. In the third and fourth years we begin to discriminate about whether a student should continue into the higher levels. This is for two reasons. First, without adequate feet, rotation in the hips, a slender body, and limber legs and torso, a child really can't do much in ballet, and more advanced ballet begins to be dangerous to attempt. Second, since the school is not a big money-making enterprise, it would be meaningless to go on if we couldn't establish an artistic level that interested *us*.

We not only had to train dancers; we also had to educate their families to understand and accept the various disciplines of ballet. One of the ways we did this was to make our instructions to the dancers more meaningful. We taught them how to feel the steps in their muscles and how to keep improving the quality of their work. As the parents saw our results and the enthusiasm of the children, they were eager to follow our direction.

I would say that contact with SAB has given us more insight into our craft, an outlet for our top students, and a curriculum to model our school after. In short, it helped us to change from a studio to a school.

EK: How about the beginners' groups?

SR: Oh! We had twenty boys that first year. The whole building would go BONG on Thursdays. I sent out notices—to public schools and so forth— that we were starting a boys' class sponsored by the School of American Ballet. Twenty-four boys showed up. We went right through them and came up with ten who stayed. They wanted big movement right away— big jumps—while we wanted them to do cou-de-pied. It was hopeless! But two got to be really good and then went into the girls' classes. One, Edward Farley, is now a soloist with Ballet West, dancing principal roles.

Eleanor kept that boys' class for years. It was a pleasure, so full of a different kind of energy. Now we teach boys and girls together. If we had more boys, we would give them regular classes with girls *and* special classes.

Note: In the spring of 1981 Rozann and Zimmerman sold the Ballet Center to a former student, Christine Schenk, who had earned Ford-sponsored local scholarships at home and who had studied at SAB under Ford-sponsored regional scholarships.

George Balanchine (shown here with Igor Stravinsky at a 1957 rehearsal of Agon) is widely regarded as the century's foremost choreographer in the world of ballet. He graduated from the Imperial Ballet School in St. Petersburg, Russia, in 1921, then served as ballet master with Serge Diaghilev's Ballets Russes from 1924 until the company was dissolved following Diaghilev's death in 1929. Coming to the United States in 1933, Balanchine founded the School of American Ballet the following year, with Lincoln Kirstein. In 1935, Balanchine, Kirstein, and Edward Warburg founded the first of several ballet companies, the American Ballet. In 1946, Balanchine and Kirstein collaborated again to found Ballet Society, a company that, as the "New York City Ballet," was invited in 1948 to join the New York City Center municipal complex. From then until his death in 1983, Balanchine served as ballet master for the company, which is now resident at the New York State Theater at Lincoln Center. He choreographed the majority of the 175 productions the company has introduced since its inception.

INTERVIEW WITH GEORGE BALANCHINE

ELIZABETH KENDALL: What was your role in the Ford Foundation's dance program?

GEORGE BALANCHINE: The Foundation asked Lincoln Kirstein and myself to suggest how some of its dance funding might be distributed. We worked very hard, and I personally went all over the country to see the existing schools. We evaluated the teachers, the way they taught, how many pupils they had and how they looked. We advised the Foundation on how to help some of the schools with scholarships.

EK: When you traveled over the country in the late fifties looking at ballet activity and ballet schools, what did you find?

GB: Almost nothing. And for several years after, all the teachers came to us [in summer Teachers' Seminars] and we showed them how we teach. I taught what I learned as a child in St. Petersburg at the Maryinsky School. (Now Moscow is the most important city in Russia. Then St. Petersburg was where you saw all the dancing. St. Petersburg was the kitchen for dance.) Now the American teachers start to be better, to imitate, to have eyes. You have to see things.

So many dancers have been trained since then, slowly. Like evolution, it takes a long time. They grow up, they dance. Then another generation comes. Some of the older ones teach.

Now we have the School [of American Ballet] and we have lots of children dancing. They watch the best dancers, they imitate, by imitating they learn—like animals, or like baby birds who learn to fly by imitating the mother bird.

EK: In the first, experimental year of the Ford Foundation dance scholarships—1961-62—Suzanne Farrell was in the group. Was she a surprise to you, coming from Cincinnati?

GB: No, not a surprise, just nicely built. She could do a few things, but she was no accomplished dancer. She learned everything here.

We didn't then, and we don't now, audition from the streets the way some ballet companies do. For the company we only take our own people, only people from our school. The rest are very good too, so we recommend them to other companies: to Europe, to American Ballet Theatre, for example.

EK: Do the young people now coming into the company appear to you to have more polish as a result of the scholarship program?

GB: We teach differently now. But in the beginning we gave scholarships too, in the evenings, to some children whose mothers brought them. Before Ford we already gave scholarships: about a hundred got free lessons. When the School of American Ballet was on Madison Avenue, we taught many people—adults—who simply studied ballet, who were not interesting material. About three hundred in all. But their fees paid for the scholarships we gave.

EK: When you were a ballet master with Diaghilev, did you ever teach?

GB: In Diaghilev's company, Cecchetti taught class. But I was teaching too while I was staging the ballets: showing how the steps should look, making sure the dancers knew how to do them. I never "became a teacher"; no, I am a person who teaches. Bad dancers "become teachers." The girls dance in the corps de ballet, then they marry, then they open a school. But the good teachers—they were first good dancers, with technique.

EK: How did the Teachers' Seminars, which began in 1960, get started?

GB: We looked at the map—all fifty states. We asked, Is anybody there? We found a few people. What I showed them was all free: four hours a day, sometimes more. How the instep is developed. How to turn. All free. Some that couldn't even pay for transportation—we paid. And they got to ask questions. "Why do you do that?" I answered, "That's what I think it is. That's what I was taught in St. Petersburg."

EK: But haven't you changed the technique you teach since your days as a student?

GB: Not changed. You adapt certain things. It's like reading Rabelais: you can't read Rabelais in the original even if you know French. He has to be translated into modern French.

EK: You once wrote in a statement at the beginning of the Ford Foundation's efforts that a program of assistance "must provide an atmosphere in which we can breathe." Did you get it?

GB: Finally. Now, of course, the Ford Foundation doesn't help us anymore. We exist by our own financing methods. We have people who support the company and people who support the school. We have everybody. And we have our own dancers. An embarrassment of riches, as they say.

EK: How did you choose the people who were sent forth from the School of American Ballet to choose the scholarship students?

GB: Sometimes you send somebody who's available. The people I send know our needs. A person like Diana Adams—I valued her opinion. And then I have a theory that if a person has short legs he will choose short-legged people—like me. If he has a short neck and large head, soon we will see short necks and large heads. But you take "Charlie's Angels"—they are tall, finely proportioned. But we don't expect them to dance. You need also ability—technique—even though people object to that idea.

EK: They object to technique?

GB: Yes, they say a dancer needs art, not technique. But technique means art in Greek.

EK: Do you have a final statement about the Ford Foundation's effect on ballet?

GB: McNeil Lowry is responsible for this. He is a wonderful man—a great man. He helped us to make lots of little companies. We continue as before. I give any company that wants them my ballets, which they can dance for free. They only have to pay a person to stage them. The earth gives free what plants need to grow.

Lisa Jackson is in her early twenties. She never held an official Ford Foundation dance scholarship; rather, she was a full-scholarship student at both the San Francisco Ballet School and the School of American Ballet after the scholarship financing was taken over directly by the schools themselves She and her generation are the beneficiaries of the "ballet network" that resulted indirectly from the Ford Foundation's dance activities begun in 1959. In 1981, Lisa Jackson joined the New York City Ballet. Here she appears in a recent City Ballet production of Debussy's Afternoon of a Faun.

INTERVIEW WITH LISA JACKSON

ELIZABETH KENDALL: Tell me about your family, and about your early dance experience.

LISA JACKSON: I was born in California, in the San Fernando Valley. I don't know why I started dancing. All little kids take things like gymnastics, piano, or ballet; I took ballet and got interested in it. My first ballet school, which I first went to when I was four-and-a-half or five, was in a suburban beach town to the south of L.A. There were a lot of dancers in it who I thought were really good, and everyone competed very hard. I wasn't "strange" because I studied ballet. A lot of kids from my high school studied at my ballet school, partly because it was right across the street from the high school. I continued to go there until I went to study in San Francisco.

EK: When did you first know that you wanted to dance?

LJ: When I was about twelve.

EK: And how did you know?

LJ: It was fun. I loved it. It was a wonderful feeling, but it was also something to work for, a challenge.

EK: Did you see much live ballet at that age?

LJ: I didn't see a lot. The first ballet I ever saw was ABT. I never saw the New York City Ballet out there in California. But I knew, even when I was growing up, that I had the body for New York City Ballet.

EK: Were you tall?

LJ: I wasn't tall, but I was really thin, They always used to tell me I should grow, but I always had extension. I guess that's how people in California thought of me: New York City Ballet, long legs, extension.

I grew up thinking that extension and lots of turns were everything. I didn't know that much about line and technique, about placing your feet, about the way your leg should move, how your arms should work—especially how your arms should work. My arms just stuck out like sticks.

EK: How did your perceptions about technique, training, and about yourself as a dancer change when you went to study in San Francisco?

LJ: The training I got, mostly from Sally Streets and Zola Dishong of the San Francisco Ballet School, was a lot better than what I'd had at home in Los Angeles.

EK: Zola was actually one of the first Ford Foundation scholarship people in 1961. And now she's a fine teacher.

LJ: I think it helped me to have people take an interest in me. It made me want to work more, not so much for myself as for them. When you're younger—I was fourteen when I went to San Francisco—you kind of work for attention.

I think I decided I really wanted to dance when I stopped working for the teacher and started working for me.

EK: But the attention that Zola gave you was of another kind?

LJ: Yes, it was a kind of suggestive correction. She would correct me and then, if I didn't work on it, she would kind of say, "Fine. Fine. You don't want to do it, fine." Then you realized what you were there for. I was there to dance, I was there on a scholarship, and if I wasn't going to take a correction, to use her help, then I shouldn't have been there.

EK: What do you suppose it is that makes a person want to work truly and carefully, to strike a clear pose instead of an approximate, half-hearted one?

LJ: I don't know. But that's just it. That's what I love so much. I love to work. I love to take classes and to know that I'm aiming for something that might not work this time, but that I'm slowly strengthening my will. I've been trying to work even when I'm tired because I know in the long run it's going to make me stronger. Even if I don't have time to take class, I'll give myself a real good hard warmup and be tired, and then go and perform being tired. It's just going to make me so much stronger.

Sometimes you go through a ballet and you think you're going to die, but knowing that you've done it before makes it easier. Because once you're on stage you have to do it. It's not like class.

EK: Why did you come to the School of American Ballet in New York when you were settled at the San Francisco Ballet School?

LJ: Because I wanted to see what SAB was like. I'd always heard that it was the best.

EK: How did you go about trying to get to the City Ballet?

LJ: There was an audition for the SAB. I had always heard about these auditions and there was a big notice up at our school, so I went, as did several other girls. It was so crowded that they took thirty people at a time. I remember not understanding how they could take people without seeing them dance. They must have known exactly what they were looking for.

EK: After your first summer at SAB you went back to California. Why?

LJ: I had been asked to come back to SAB, but my parents decided that I had to finish high school and get a little bit of college before I could come back. I was torn between the two points of view, but I talked to SAB and they said it was okay, so I came back the next January.

EK: How about the teachers in SAB since you've been here full-time? Have they been important?

LJ: They are all important—every one. They all teach in different ways.

EK: Has Mr. Balanchine been teaching?

LJ: I've only had two weeks of classes from him in all. He taught for a week when I first became an apprentice.

EK: What was he like?

LJ: Hard. So hard. He makes you work until you think you are going to die. But you've got to do it. You just keep going.

EK: Are there certain dancers in City Ballet that you have been watching to learn things from?

LJ: Oh, everybody. I stand in the wings every performance of everything. People are always teasing me, saying "Don't you get tired of watching?" Never. Because you can see the same ballet six thousand times, and every time you'll see something different. Maybe something you can apply to yourself someday.

EK: Do you think you could be happy staying in the City Ballet for a long time?

LJ: Yes, forever!

Suzanne Farrell received a Ford Foundation dance scholarship in 1960 and joined the New York City Ballet in 1961—at the age of sixteen. She is one of the great ballerinas of our time. Here she appears with Peter Martins in a 1976 performance of Allegro Brillante, *choreographed by Balanchine with music by Tchaikovsky.*

Interview with Suzanne Farrell

ELIZABETH KENDALL: How did you come to be interested in dancing?

SUZANNE FARRELL: As far as I know, no one in our family had ever been in the arts, but for some reason my mother liked dancing. She had wanted to dance, but her mother—my grandmother—wouldn't let her because it was too expensive. I guess my mother said—looking into the future—that if she ever was in the same position, she'd make dancing available to *her* children. She'd let her daughters dance if they wanted to.

EK: You weren't made to take lessons?

SF: No, she didn't force us—me or my two older sisters—to do anything. If you were interested you could take it. It was available. Even if she couldn't afford it she would find a way. My older sister started dancing and was quite good. The next sister, who wasn't physically inclined at all, became a pianist, and was also very good. We were poor. I don't say we were as poor as the poorest, but my mother was spending all the money we had on our art lessons. Fortunately we were talented enough to get scholarships.

EK: What did you think you might want to do before you started to dance?

SF: I didn't have that much life before that. I was always tall and skinny and very flexible. I did a lot of acrobatics.

EK: When did you first think that dancing was something you could do all your life?

SF: When I was about twelve years old. My teacher at the Cincinnati Conservatory of Music was Marian LaCour, and she was very smart. My sister was in the advanced class, so instead of just letting me hang around while my sister took her class, she said "Why don't you take class also?" It was way above me, but it was a wonderful change. Before long I was trying to do things that I couldn't do, and before long I was doing some things that I thought I couldn't do, that by rights I shouldn't have been able to do. So she said, "Why don't you just be the understudy for the older group?" They would do concerts around town, so as it happened I had to go on one day and it was just the most wonderful experience to dance with a real orchestra in front of real people who weren't your mother and father.

EK: What made you come to New York?

SF: My mother had read in *Dance* magazine or somewhere about how the Ford Foundation was thinking of giving a grant or whatever for dance training.

She showed the article to my teacher and asked her to see if she couldn't arrange to have someone come to Cincinnati. My teacher at the time thought she had a pupil more talented than I was, so she did arrange to have someone come. As it turned out, the person who came was Diana Adams, a ballerina from the New York City Ballet.

EK: What did Diana Adams see in you?

SF: Diana saw that I was very musical, that my nature was aggressive or, rather, not aggressive but venturesome. She didn't say anything to me, though I did get her autograph. I guess she said something to my teacher and got my name turned in. All I know is that I came to New York and I had a special audition with Mr. B.—Mr. Balanchine—and none of the other kids did. Diana must have thought there was something special about me to merit having an audition with me privately.

EK: What was it like, that special audition?

SF: After the letter from SAB arrived in April or May, we sold all our things and stayed in my sister's apartment in Cincinnati until well into the summer. Then we drove east in our broken-down Ford with a U-Haul trailer behind us and installed ourselves in the Ansonia Hotel. The audition happened to be on my fifteenth birthday, in August.

I remember my mother and I were sitting on a red vinyl-covered bench when Mr. Balanchine came in with his string tie on. I remember Mother saying, "My God, there he is."

When we were alone in the studio he said, "Well, what are you going to do?"

"Well, what do you mean?" I said. I guess he expected a routine. I was terrified. "I could hum my recital dance—as I go along," I said. He must have thought, "Gee, this girl is musical if she can hum!"

Then he said, "All right, take your shoe off. Point your foot." He tried to bend my toes back with me pushing against him, to see how strong my feet were. He didn't say much, and I said even less. I was totally in the dark. I just got dressed, and then my mother and I went to Schrafft's. I didn't know anything until the letter came a day or so later saying that I had gotten into C Class at SAB.

EK: What did you think of the school?

SF: I remember seeing part of the summer school going on—so many girls, and all so good. I thought I didn't stand a chance. So all of the time I lived in fear. Of course, the fact that I, unlike the other scholarship kids, was staying with my mother and sister didn't give me time to fraternize with the others. But it was to my advantage to be with my family.

When I came with my mother and sister to New York, the three of us lived in a one-room apartment; we never even unpacked our boxes. We had a baby grand piano for my sister, a trundle bed, and a hotplate. And the plumbing was always going out so we'd have to go to the Automat to go to the bathroom. My mother had to work at night because we only had the one bed, which had room for only one or two people. We would do our homework in the afternoons while Mom was asleep. And we thought it was wonderful. We were happy.

It's important to be young while you can. I got into the company when I was very young—sixteen. Yet onstage we're professionals. It doesn't matter that we haven't lived, haven't been kissed by a boy.

EK: Would you tell me something about your experiences later as a Ford Foundation scout, auditioning scholarship students, and as a teacher at SAB?

SF: It was very difficult. Mr. Balanchine gave me the state of Ohio. I was nineteen, twenty, twenty-one—still just getting things going as a performer. Mr. B. wanted me to teach at the same time. At first it made me feel like a has-been, but ultimately it's made me so much better as a dancer. I know the kids that I teach will see me dance in the evenings, and I have to live up to what they expect.

When I went out into Ohio to audition, I learned how awful things were as recently as sixteen or seventeen years ago. In some places ballet was just a racket. People made a lot of money. Lots of cute, pretty little girls were getting ruined. It was sad to have to go through the sham of auditioning when you saw there was nothing there. But I would give them a class; I didn't want anybody to go away from the situation hating ballet. When you finally saw a kid who could stand up it was wonderful.

Now, even though ballet standards are better, becoming a ballerina is just as hard. I tell my students that it's not enough to be tall, pretty, and strong, with high extensions and a good jump. Mr. Balanchine has had people like that in his life for years. You have to have more—whether it's soul, musicality, simplicity. Whatever the "more" is, you have to find it.

Ford Foundation Assistance to American Dance 1959–1983

BALLET

Professional Training

Ballet Society, Inc.
Three-year program of regional scholarships for study at the School of American Ballet and the School of the San Francisco Ballet (1959, 1961) $ 162,500

School of American Ballet
Planning and development of a program to assist the national and regional development of performance and training in ballet (1963) 60,000

Ballet development program
To strengthen permanent performing and instructional resources in the United States

School of American Ballet
Ten-year program to strengthen the school as a national center for advanced professional training (1964) 2,425,000

Cooperative system between the school and ballet teachers in different parts of the country to improve the professional preparation of promising young dancers (1964) 1,500,000

Professional training program and an operating reserve fund (1974) 2,010,000

Capital grant for the establishment of a Ford Foundation Scholarship Fund (1983) 250,000

Houston Ballet
Training program (1964) 173,750

Strengthening Artistic Resources

Strengthening professional ballet companies
In December 1963 the Foundation announced a many-faceted program to strengthen professional ballet in the United States. The following grants have been made under that program:

Boston Ballet (1964, 1966, 1969, 1970)	769,000
Dance Theatre of Harlem (1970, 1971, 1972, 1973, 1976, 1978, 1979, 1983)	4,062,365
Joffrey Ballet (1965, 1966, 1968, 1972, 1974, 1983)	3,798,500
National Ballet (1964, 1971)	628,500
New York City Ballet (1964, 1973, 1974)	2,500,000
Pennsylvania Ballet (1964, 1966, 1968, 1971, 1973)	4,870,722
San Francisco Ballet (1964)	644,000
Utah Civic Ballet (Ballet West) (1964)	175,000

Stabilization/cash reserve program
In 1971 the Foundation began a program of grants designed to improve and stabilize the financial position of nonprofit performing arts companies. Ballet companies that have received such grants are:

American Ballet Theatre (1972, 1982)	1,150,000
Ballet West (1971)	287,491
Boston Ballet (1972)	470,460
Eliot Feld Ballet (1981)	280,000
Joffrey Ballet (1974, 1978)	1,000,000 *
Houston Ballet (1973, 1981)	353,582
New York City Ballet (1974)	2,700,000
North Carolina Dance Theatre (1979)	96,992
San Francisco Ballet (1976)	926,281

*In 1979 the Joffrey Ballet received a program-related investment of $50,000 in the form of a cash-flow guarantee. (Program-related investments are capital funds invested in enterprises that advance philanthropic purposes.)

MODERN DANCE

Performance and Preservation of the Repertoire of Modern Dance

Martha Graham Foundation for Contemporary Dance
Recording of a new score for a dance work (1965)
and filming of eight works from Martha Graham's
repertoire (1968) $150,000

New York City performance seasons for major modern dance companies
Albar Theatre Arts [Billy Rose Theater](1968)   100,000
Brooklyn Academy of Music (1968, 1969)   266,000
City Center of Music and Drama (1968)   285,000

Chicago Dance Foundation
Annual dance festivals (1971)   53,846

American Dance Festival
Connecticut College (1972, 1974, 1975)   180,600
Restructuring: American Dance Festival (1978)   30,000
    North Carolina School of the Arts
    (1978)   10,000
General Support (1980)   150,000

TAG Foundation
Performances by small dance companies under the
Dance Umbrella (1976, 1977, 1980)   261,682

Foundation-managed project
Joint marketing and subscription campaign for the
New York City season of five major modern dance
companies: Alvin Ailey, Merce Cunningham, José
Limón, Murray Louis, and Alwin Nikolais (1979)   120,000

Nikolais/Louis Foundation for Dance
Expansion of dance marketing consortium (1981)   4,000

Walker Art Center
New Dance U.S.A., a contemporary dance festival
(1981)   10,000

Professional Training

Dance Theatre Foundation (Alvin Ailey City Center Dance Theater)
Living stipends and tuition assistance for students
enrolled at the American Dance Center, the official
school of the Dance Theatre Foundation (1974)   189,600

Strengthening Artistic Resources

Stabilization/cash reserve grants
Cunningham Dance Foundation (1978, 1979)   241,202*
Dance Theatre Foundation [Alvin Ailey City Center
    Dance Theater] (1974)   460,923
Murray Louis Dance Group (1978)   119,691*
Nikolais Dance Group (1978)   160,758*
Paul Taylor Dance Foundation (1978)   155,140*
Twyla Tharp Dance Foundation (1979)   167,872**

Management assistance
Harry's Foundation [Senta Driver] (1981)   15,000
Street Dance Productions [Gail Conrad] (1981)   15,000

RESEARCH AND DEVELOPMENT

Columbia University
Choreometrics Project, a study by anthropologist
Alan Lomax of a worldwide sample of dances, from
tribal dances to ballet (1969, 1971) $ 86,729

Dance Notation Bureau (New York City)
Administrative support for the practice and development of recording the details of dance movements
by trained observers (1970, 1975)   125,000

*Includes operating support
**Includes support for the development of a full-length dance work

Placing dance notation experts with selected dance companies (1981)   60,000

Lincoln Center for the Performing Arts
Development of techniques of live telecasting of ballet (1974)   126,985

American Dance Machine (New York City)
Administrative support for the reconstruction of choreographic works from outstanding Broadway musicals, for training, and for performances (1979)   45,240

SCHOLARSHIP AND CRITICISM

Program for Reporters, Editors, and Critics
Fellowships to extend professional experience: Renee Renouf Hall, Richard O. Martin (1965) $ 13,320

New York Public Library
For an automated book catalog of the library's dance collection (1965, 1967)   141,000

The Eakins Press Foundation
Completion of a bibliography of the writings of Lincoln Kirstein (1978)   4,000

KCET-TV (Los Angeles)
Videotaping Agnes de Mille's *Conversations About the Dance* (1978)   25,000

City Center of Music and Drama [for the New York City Ballet] (1979, 1983)
Preparation and publication of *Choreography by George Balanchine* (New York: Eakins Press)   35,000

California State University
Documentary film on American dance pioneer Hanya Holm (1983)   39,220

Dance Perspectives Foundation (New York City)
Preparation of an *International Encyclopedia of Dance* (1983)   31,167

INDIVIDUAL GRANTS

Grants-in-Aid for administrative interns at the New York City Ballet: Carol Deschamps (1963–64), Harvey Lichtenstein (1964–65), Sunny C. Asch (1969–70) $19,748

Travel and study awards: Nancy White Dennis, for a book on *The Red Shoes*; Karen Kanner, for a collaborative project involving Western and Greek dance technicians; Olga Maynard, for a history of the School of American Ballet; Donald McDonagh, for a biography of Martha Graham; Nancy Reynolds, for a history of the New York City Ballet; Robert Rodham, for visits to ballet companies and schools in the United States and Western Europe.   65,754

OTHER GRANTS RELATED TO THE DANCE

Since 1966, the Foundation has supported a number of activities in education, research, technical assistance, and the support of multiple arts organizations. Many include but are not exclusively devoted to matters concerning dance.

Arts and Education

North Carolina School of the Arts
Training of high school and college students in music, drama, and dance (1966) $1,500,000
Cash reserve/stabilization grant (1979)   139,008
Program-related investment: bridge loan to complete construction of the Roger L. Stevens Center for the Performing Arts (1982)   1,000,000

Performing Arts Workshop (San Francisco)
Drama and dance training for disadvantaged youths
(1967, 1969)   162,500

Harlem School of the Arts
Training in theater and dance (1969)   262,000
Construction of new training facilities (1975)   600,000

Henry Street Settlement (New York City)
Training in film and dance (1970)   70,000

Newark Community Center of the Arts (New
Jersey)
Instruction in music, dance, and drama (1970, 1975,
1979, 1980)   554,423

The George Washington University
Workshops for Careers in the Arts: training in visual
and performing arts for talented students from public
high schools in Washington, D.C. (1973, 1976)   524,500

Senehen, Inc. (New York City)
Partial support of the dance component of "Artists-
in-Schools" (1977)   22,000

Association of Schools in the Arts (New York
City)
Accreditation of professional training schools in
theater and dance (1977, 1978, 1979, 1980)   112,851

National Dance Institute
Dance training in New York City schools (1978,
1980)   42,500

ArtsConnection (New York City)
Training of gifted, disadvantaged children in dance,
ballet, and acrobatics at the Alvin Ailey Dance Center and the New York School for Circus Arts/Big
Apple Circus (1981)   50,000

Research, Development, and Public Policy Studies

The Finances of the Performing Arts
Foundation-managed survey of the economics and
financing of 166 professional nonprofit resident
theaters, operas, symphonies, ballets, and modern
dance companies (1970, 1971, 1972, 1974, 1975)   1,280,150

Multiple Arts Organizations

Affiliate Artists (New York City)
Residencies for young singers, dancers, musicians,
and theatrical artists in communities across the
United States (1973)   700,000

Brooklyn Academy of Music
Production and touring of the NEXT WAVE, music,
dance, and theater events that stress collaboration
among major American avant-garde performing artists (1983)   300,000

                                  Total $42,578,552

Elizabeth Kendall has written extensively on dance and American culture. She is the author of *Where She Danced* (Knopf, 1979)—about the birth of American modern dance—and of a forthcoming book on Hollywood romantic comedy in the 1930s. Ms. Kendall lives in New York City.

The New York City Ballet performs the Stravinsky Violin Concerto as choreographed by George Balanchine.

Design: Ruth Neumann
Typography: Columbia Publishing Company, Inc.
Printing: Village Craftsmen

Photo Research: Libby Watterson
Photographs: *Where no credit is listed, photographs were obtained from the institution mentioned in the caption.* Cover — Harvey Edwards; inside covers, 43, 48 — Paul Kolnik; 8 (right), 29 — San Francisco Ballet; 8 (left) — The Historical Society of Pennsylvania; 11, 13, 17, 18, 23, 26, 38, 44, 50 (below left), 59, 66, 72 — Martha Swope; 16 — Robert Clayton/Ballet West; 21 — The Rank Organisation; 34 — Charlie Erickson; 37 — Herbert Migdoll; 49 — Jay Anderson; 51 — David Lubarsky; 52 (right) — Lois Greenfield; 53 (lower left) — Jack Mitchell; 53 (left) — Ken Kay; 53 (below) — Tom Caravaglia; 54 — Nancy Moran; 63 — Ilene S. Adler; 69 — Steven Caras.